A Reflective Framework
for Living with Clarity and Care

V.I.T.A.L.
AGING

JOHN SINUES

AFTER THE BLACKOUT

Moving Through the World with

V.I.T.A.L.

JOHN SINUES

Author of

V.I.T.A.L. AGING

A Reflective Framework for
Living with Clarity and Care

V.I.T.A.L. AGING

Disclaimer: This book is offered as a reflective and educational work. It is not intended to replace professional medical, psychological, or fitness advice. Readers should consult qualified professionals regarding individual health, movement, or treatment decisions. The author assumes no responsibility for the application of the information contained herein.

ISBN: 979-8-9952993-0-1 (Paperback)

Library of Congress Control Number: 2026906760

Subjects: Self-Help / Personal Growth / General; Psychology / Developmental / Adulthood & Aging

Cover and Interior Design: Jennifer Federico Stimson

First Edition: April 2026

Printed in the United States of America

Dedication

To my parents, Vincent and Elena Sinues, whose love was quiet but unwavering, whose sacrifices were immeasurable, whose lives—lived with dignity, resilience, and grace—became the blueprint for everything I now hold dear.

Your passing opened a space I never expected: a stillness filled with sorrow, silence, and the sacred permission to finally listen. In that pause, a lens shifted. What once felt like loss became focus. And from that focus came this work.

This book is a thank you—quiet, reflective, and alive with intention. You gave me the time not just to grieve but to observe, to grow, to become. I wish you were here to see it. But in every word, every breath, and every data point on this journey—you are.

These pages are my margins—like those
I once filled with borrowed ink.

A reminder that even in the most confined spaces,
there is always room to write your own story.

AUTHOR'S NOTE

Welcome. I wrote this book because I needed a map for living when choice felt limited. The pages that follow mix story, data, and simple practices that steadied me after a blackout and through confinement. You won't find a one-size-fits-all plan here—only tools you can adapt. Try the Three-Minute Frame Reset in chapter 1. If it helps, try the Daily V.I.T.A.L. Rhythm for a week. If it doesn't, try something else. My hope is that this book becomes a companion: a place to return when you need clarity, a set of small experiments to test, and a language to share with others. Start where you are. Move at your pace. You're not alone in this.

Take what serves you and let the rest wait for another season.

This morning, my body battery[1] peaked near ninety—enough to remind me that recovery matters.

Yesterday was full of motion—pickleball rallies, shoreline stretches, deep laughter with friends. By nightfall my mind was racing; ideas for Project V.I.T.A.L. came fast and scattered. Today I choose stillness as refinement. Someday a future version of me will sit with the raw materials of this life—journal entries, photographs, heart-rate logs—and unpack them with care. That analysis will illuminate the movements I took and the pillars they revealed.

This book is both memoir and mirror. It grew from lived practice and careful observation. V.I.T.A.L. didn't arrive as a single insight; it emerged gradually, like a photograph in developer fluid. What follows is a map of how I want to live—rooted in movement, meaning, and the small acts that hold us steady.

---

1   This is referring to Garmin's Body Battery, a feature found on many Garmin smartwatches that estimates your body's energy levels throughout the day—kind of like a fuel gauge for your physical and mental readiness.

It's important to say this plainly: this is not a program. It isn't meant to be read in a straight line, and it isn't a manual for fixing aging. It's a companionable walk through capability, loss, and the slow return to agency. You're welcome to skip, pause, circle back, or enter wherever you feel drawn. Returning later is success, not failure. This book is meant to meet you where you are, not pull you somewhere you're not ready to go. If you find yourself slowing down, doubling back, or needing space, that's part of the work. This book is meant to move with you, not ahead of you.

You may also notice the tone is steady and observational. That's intentional. The story is told with the same calm distance that helped me move through it. THE AIM ISN'T TO DRAMATIZE THE PAST, BUT TO OFFER A CLEAR, GROUNDED VIEW OF IT—A POSTURE THAT GIVES YOU ROOM TO BREATHE, NOTICE, AND FIND YOUR OWN PACE INSIDE THESE PAGES. The calmness you'll feel here reflects how I lived through these moments—measured, steady, and sometimes from a slight distance. That distance isn't detachment; it's how I found clarity, and it's the space that allows your own story to unfold alongside mine.

CONTENTS

START HERE

(with Reader Promise)

If you're opening this book, something in your life is shifting. You may be standing at a hinge moment of your own—between what was and what comes next. Wherever you are, begin gently.

This book isn't a program to master. It's a companion for the seasons when life narrows and you need a way to widen the frame again. You don't have to read it in order. **START WHERE THE LIGHT FEELS STRONGEST**—with story, with context, with the pillars, or with the closing pages that steady you.

READER PROMISE:

This book will meet you where you are. It will offer clarity without pressure, structure without rigidity, and practices that honor your pace, your season, and your dignity. You will not be asked to transform overnight. You will be invited to move—slowly, honestly, and with intention—toward a life that feels more aligned and more your own.

Take what resonates. Leave the rest in the margins.

Return when you need grounding.

Skip ahead when you need clarity.

Circle back when you need courage.

This book won't tell you who to become.

It will help you notice who you already are—and what you're ready to carry forward.

Begin anywhere.

Begin softly.

Begin with one small act.

The spiral starts here.

HOW TO USE THIS BOOK

This book isn't a program or a prescription. It doesn't offer steps, solutions, or a path to follow. It's a reflective companion shaped by lived experience—a way of seeing rather than a set of instructions. You're invited to move through it at your own pace, noticing what resonates, setting aside what doesn't, and allowing your own clarity to guide you forward.

This book is designed to meet you where you are. You can read it straight through or enter at the chapter that speaks to your current season. The front matter offers several ways to begin: Start Here provides grounding, A Map Of What's To Come gives you an overview of the journey, and A Gentle Beginning offers simple practices you can use immediately.

Each chapter blends story, reflection, and movement-based reflections. You'll find Shutter Checks and small prompts throughout—use them as gentle pauses, not assignments. The V.I.T.A.L. framework unfolds gradually, and Appendix F gathers its applications in one place if you prefer to explore the tools directly.

The book closes with a Final Reflection, a moment to integrate what you've learned before you step back into your own life. Move through these pages at your own pace. Begin where the light feels strongest.

USING THE GLOSSARY

To support your journey, the book includes a V.I.T.A.L. Glossary. It is more than a list of definitions—it is a companion, a decoder ring, and a map.

- **Quick Reference (Five Pillars)**: Begin here. Vitality, Intention, Tenacity, Alignment, and Longevity are the compass points of the framework.
- **Synergies & Interactions**: Explore how the pillars connect. These entries show the living relationships that give the framework coherence.
- **Supporting Terms & Metaphors**: Dive deeper into photography, data science, and movement science. Each entry offers context and imagery to help you translate metaphors into practice.

Return to the glossary as you read. Let it clarify unfamiliar terms, spark reflection, and guide application. It is not an appendix to skim once but a living tool to revisit—helping you carry forward the language of intentional aging.

DIFFERENT WAYS READERS ENGAGE WITH THIS BOOK

If You're Reading as an Individual

- Many readers begin with chapters 1 and 5 to understand the V.I.T.A.L. pillars.
- You might explore the Micro-Experiments and Pillar Pulse Checks to build daily routines.
- Reflect with the Postscript and Epilogue to explore how movement and meaning can coexist—even after crisis.

If You're Reading as a Caregiver and Family

- Read the Postscript to understand how mental-health crises can escalate—and how to prevent them.
- You might explore the Crisis Directive Template to cocreate a plan with your loved one.
- The Movement Domain Scores can help you to tailor physical routines that support emotional regulation.

- Share reflection prompts across generations to spark conversations about legacy and resilience.

If You Support Others Professionally

- Begin with the Postscript and Afterword to hear a lived experience of crisis and recovery.
- You might explore the Co-Response Checklist to explore alternatives to escalation.
- Consider how V.I.T.A.L. can inform trauma-informed care, de-escalation, and post-crisis support.

If You Teach or Facilitate

- Adapt reflection questions as group discussion starters.
- You might explore the Micro-Experiments as classroom or workshop activities.
- Frame the pillars as a shared language for resilience and intentional aging.

If You Lead in Community Spaces

- Apply the framework in senior centers, nonprofits, or faith communities.
- You might explore the pillars to design programs that blend movement, connection, and legacy-building.
- Encourage members to create their own "What I Carry Forward" rituals.

A NOTE ON ADVERSITY

Aging with intention doesn't mean aging without adversity. Many readers will face chronic health setbacks, financial constraints, caregiving demands, or societal messages that diminish their sense of worth. These realities are not footnotes—they are central to the human experience.

The V.I.T.A.L. framework is not a rigid prescription but a living compass. It's designed to meet you where you are, offering adaptable strategies that honor your circumstances while inviting movement, connection, and agency. Whether you're navigating grief, rebuilding after a crisis, or simply seeking steadier ground, this book is for you.

This book is not a prescription. It's a companion. It doesn't promise ease, but it does offer clarity. V.I.T.A.L. is not about perfection— it's about presence. It's about reclaiming agency, even in the face of uncertainty.

READER INVITATION

This book is meant to walk beside you. The stories, research, and reflections are here to spark movement and meaning, but the real work happens in your own life. The glossary offers language to guide you, the pillars provide a compass, and the synergies remind you that strength is found in connection.

You may find yourself returning to certain passages, circling back to the glossary, or pausing with a reflection prompt when life feels unsettled. That is the design. V.I.T.A.L. is not about finishing—it is about living with presence.

Carry forward what resonates. Adapt what you need. Leave space for discovery. And remember: Hope is sustained when we name it, agency is strengthened when we practice it, and dignity is honored when we live it. This book is yours to inhabit, and the framework is yours to make your own.

Live V.I.T.A.L.: with energy to move, intention to guide, persistence to endure, balance to sustain, and perspective to carry forward.

A GENTLE BEGINNING

- Move your body for ten minutes (walk, stretch, breathe deeply).
- Write one sentence about what matters most today.
- Keep one small routine (drink water, tidy a corner, journal a line).
- Pause once and ask: Does this choice reflect my values?
- Do one thing your future self will thank you for (call a friend, plant a seed, save a note, rest).

These five practices are your entry point. To deepen the practice, continue with the Daily V.I.T.A.L. Rhythm, where each pillar is explored in full detail.

V.I.T.A.L. AGING

A DAILY V.I.T.A.L. RHYTHM

Use this five-step check-in as a daily rhythm. Keep it short, keep it consistent.

V	Move for a few minutes (stretch, walk, breathe).
I	Write one guiding sentence for the day.
T	Repeat one small act of consistency.
A	Pause midday and ask: *Am I living my values?*
L	End the day with one act your future self will thank you for.

One check-in at a time builds the habit. Repeat daily, and let presence grow.

A MAP OF WHAT'S TO COME

A brief guide to the journey ahead

This book unfolds in two movements:

Part one helps you see clearly.
Part two helps you live deliberately.

You can read straight through or enter wherever your life is asking for attention. This roadmap offers a simple orientation to the emotional and practical terrain ahead.

PART ONE: SEEING CLEARLY

Chapter 1—The Blackout: Why Now?

You begin at the hinge moment—the rupture that forces a new kind of noticing.

You may come away with: a grounding practice and the first language for understanding your own "blackout" moments.

Chapter 2—Motion Steadies the "E" in Emotion

Movement becomes medicine. You explore how physical motion regulates emotional turbulence.

You may come away with: simple, repeatable drills that reconnect body and mind.

Chapter 3—Movement Mindset

You learn how small, consistent actions shift your internal narrative and identity.

You may come away with: a mindset that favors momentum over perfection.

Chapter 4—Mindset and Metrics

You explore the role of data, measurement, and reflection—how numbers can illuminate patterns without becoming a cage.

You may come away with: a way to track progress that supports, rather than pressures, your growth.

PART TWO: LIVING DELIBERATELY

Chapter 5—The Pillars of V.I.T.A.L.

The framework comes into full view. Each pillar—Vitality, Intention, Tenacity, Alignment, Longevity—receives its own chapter.

You may come away with: a living system you can adapt to your season of life.

Chapter 6—The Hinge Generation

You widen the lens to a generational context—how we inherit patterns, pressures, and possibilities.

You may come away with: a deeper understanding of your place in the long arc of family, culture, and time.

CLOSING SECTIONS

Afterword—Grief to Generativity

A reflection on how crisis becomes contribution.

Postscript—What I Carry Forward

A look at what remains after rupture and what becomes possible.

Epilogue—Roots and Branches

A meditation on lineage, belonging, and the quiet work of repair.

Coda

A final tightening of the frame—what endures, what softens, what continues.

Appendices and Resources

These are your practical companions—frameworks, templates, scorecards, reflection pages, and glossaries designed to help you translate insight into action. Use them when you want structure, language, or a way to steady yourself through practice.

Final Reflection

A moment of integration before the last closing lines

You may come away with: a sense of readiness, clarity, and agency as you step beyond the page.

HOW TO USE THIS ROADMAP

Let it help you sense the arc.
Let it show you where you might want to begin.
Let it remind you that this book is not a race—it's a companion.

Enter wherever the light feels strongest.

PART ONE

SEEING CLEARLY

CHAPTER 1

THE BLACKOUT: WHY NOW?

{ a frame goes black }

The blackout was the moment my body gave way—the shutter slammed, the frame went dark. Months later that collapse had rippled outward into a crisis that took my freedom; incarceration made survival immediate, not theoretical.

In those first days I learned survival was more than food or shelter. It was rhythm: the small, repeatable motions that kept a nervous system from unspooling. It was agency: the tiny choices that reclaimed a sense of self. It was presence: a morning stretch, a sentence scrawled on scrap paper, a counted breath between the hours. Those small acts were lifelines.

What began as necessity became method. The practices that steadied me in a closet-size cell—breath, routine, a margin to write in—later formed the bones of V.I.T.A.L. Aging: a framework that turns collapse into renewal. This is a story not about what broke me but about what held when everything else was stripped away.

This is where the aperture narrows, and the story begins in the moment everything changed.

INTRODUCTION: AGING AS A PRACTICE, NOT A PROBLEM

We are taught to fear aging—as decline, as irrelevance, as the slow erosion of our vitality. But what if aging could be something more? What if it were a training ground for deeper purpose, wiser alignment, and holistic strength?

V.I.T.A.L. Aging reframes aging not as something to endure but as something to embrace. It asks us to train not just for lifespan but for healthspan—the vibrant years when our bodies and spirits are most alive.

Each pillar offers a new lens:

- Vitality – Energy for life through movement, recovery, and rhythm.
- Intention – Living in alignment with our core values.
- Tenacity – Building resilience through adversity.
- Alignment – Cultivating presence and attention.
- Longevity – Creating meaning in how we live and what we leave behind.

Each principle builds not a system but a way of seeing—a viewfinder for the soul. What emerges is less an instruction manual than a living map, refined through trial, movement, and listening.

THERE WAS A TIME WHEN THE WALLS AROUND ME BECAME BOTH FRAME AND TEACHER. WITHIN THAT NARROW SPACE, I LEARNED HOW LIGHT STILL FINDS ITS WAY THROUGH SMALL OPENINGS—HOW BREATH CAN EXPAND EVEN WHEN THE BODY CANNOT MOVE FAR. Constraint revealed contrast: what was necessary, what was noise. That lesson stayed with me long after the doors opened. Freedom, I learned, begins with how we see.

This necessary skill—the ability to hold the frame steady and seek the light amid the shadows—is not a lesson reserved only for a life crisis. It is the defining daily challenge of our generation. We are the pivot point in human history—raised on the weight of the analog world and thrust into the speed of the digital one. We carry the endurance of scarcity and the adaptability of abundance. We are the **Hinge Generation**.

The Fulcrum: Where Analog Weight Meets Digital Light

From Collapse to Clarity. The shift wasn't sudden. It was more like an aperture opening—gradual, almost imperceptible, until light began to reenter. GRIEF HAD HOLLOWED THE CENTER, BUT IN THAT EMPTINESS, SOMETHING STEADY BEGAN TO TAKE SHAPE: THE AWARENESS THAT SURVIVAL ISN'T A RETURN TO WHAT WAS BUT A REORIENTATION TOWARD WHAT REMAINS. I didn't expect the moment to arrive in the parking lot of a China Buffet.

Here's where the story narrows into a single moment.

It was the day of my mother's funeral. Andi and I sat in the car, hands quiet, hearts full, steeling ourselves to reenter the hum of grief and family. I turned and said softly, "I'm not ready." A beat later, I collapsed—overtaken by something deeper than fatigue.

In photography, we learn that overexposure erases detail. That day, grief yanked the shutter closed. My life paused mid-sentence. The car tilted in a slow, deliberate way, as if the world were exhaling without me. Andi steadied me, one hand cradling my head. The edges of the moment softened, but the center stayed sharp.

Yet in that darkness, the seed of V.I.T.A.L. was planted—a commitment not just to live longer but to live clearer.

From Deferral to Renewal. The next wake-up call came wrapped in data.

This wasn't the only wake-up call.

A friend—a data scientist specializing in predictive maintenance for Navy vessels—spends her weekdays parsing vibration logs and thermal curves to prevent catastrophic failures at sea. One weekend, mid-pickleball match, she felt a faint sting in her wrist during an overhead smash. She brushed it off as weekend wear. Two more games, some water, and a shrug later, she was back in motion. But by Monday, torquing a bolt during hull inspection triggered a jolt of pain. She was benched—from both the deck and the court—for weeks.

It wasn't the game that hurt her. It was neglect. The decision to defer.

In her professional life, she knows the stakes of inaction. A small deviation in engine vibration—if left unaddressed—can become a million-dollar repair or, worse, a mid-sea failure. The term she uses is *deferred maintenance*. Ignore the signals too long, and the system degrades beneath you.

The same applies to our bodies.

We push off recovery until after the next deadline. We put off movement until the weather changes. We postpone therapy, sleep, reflection—assuming *later* will show up with better bandwidth. We treat well-being like an unfunded liability—until the invoice arrives with interest.

But the truth is: We are running a personal deficit, and like the US federal one—now exceeding \$35 trillion[2]—it grows quietly, invisibly, until it can't be ignored. Every skipped walk, every numbed ache, every delayed check-in adds interest. And like any debt, the cost compounds quietly until it can't be ignored.

Now let's ground this in the numbers that mirror what so many of us already feel.

Here's the landscape we're actually living in.

- Nearly 30% of adults over age 65 report difficulty walking just three city blocks.[3]

---

2   US Department of the Treasury. Debt to the Penny. Washington, DC: U.S. Department of the Treasury. https://fiscaldata.treasury.gov/datasets/debt-to-the-penny.

3   Centers for Disease Control and Prevention. Disability and Functioning Among Older Adults: National Health Interview Survey, 2020. Atlanta, GA: CDC, 2020.

- One in four Americans age 65+ falls each year—often due to preventable muscle loss and decreased mobility.[4]
- More than two-thirds (69%) of seniors reported feeling lonely at least half the time, with physical disability or lack of mobility cited as the top cause.[5]
- After age 30, adults lose an estimated 3–8% of muscle mass per decade unless countered with strength training.[6]
- Over 85% of older adults have at least one chronic condition, and nearly 60% have two or more.[7]
- Yet only 15% of adults age 65+ meet recommended guidelines for strength, balance, and flexibility training.[8]

Like a ship that skips drydock, we drift toward dysfunction while waving it off as "just aging."

But aging isn't the enemy—neglect is.

We negotiate with ourselves while the joints seize and energy leaks. Like a nation facing crumbling infrastructure, we can't out-hustle chronic depletion.

This is where the data becomes personal.

Movement is not a luxury. It's infrastructure.
Recovery is not indulgence. It's maintenance.

---

4   National Council on Aging. Get the Facts on Falls Prevention. Arlington, VA: National Council on Aging. https://www.ncoa.org/article/get-the-facts-on-falls-prevention.

5   U.S. News & World Report. How Senior Living Communities Reduce Loneliness and Improve Senior Health: 2025 U.S. News Survey Report. May 2025. https://health.usnews.com/best-senior-living/articles/how-senior-living-communities-reduce-illness-and-improve-senior-health-survey.

6   Mitchell, W. K., et al. Sarcopenia, Dynapenia, and the Impact of Advancing Age on Skeletal Muscle Size and Strength; A Quantitative Review. Frontiers in Physiology 3 (2012): 260. https://doi.org/10.3389/fphys.2012.00260.

7   McAllister, Robert. 10 Statistics About Chronic Disease in Seniors You Need to Know for 2025. NCHstats, January 2025. https://nchstats.com/statistics-chronic-disease-seniors.

8   Centers for Disease Control and Prevention. Physical Activity Guidelines for Americans. 2nd ed. Washington, DC: US Department of Health and Human Services, 2018.

Aging well means reversing the logic of deferral. It means treating your body not in a harsh or mechanical way—but in the sense that your well-being deserves care, attention, and maintenance.

It's time to stop borrowing from tomorrow. The invoice always arrives.

Now let's bring this back to the body.

From Data to Daily Life. This book is more than a framework—it's a mirror. A gentle prompt to stop editing ourselves out of our own story.

Aging with intention is not about denying decline—it's about making meaning from it. V.I.T.A.L. is a practice of refactoring—trading outdated code for living syntax, rebooting the scripts we've inherited. Our bodies are dashboards. Every ache a query, every step a new entry, every breath a signal.

And just like data science, clarity starts with observation.

We don't need monumental change to begin. A ten-minute walk at sunrise resets your ISO. A single yoga breath rebalances exposure. A foam roll uncovers tension that was hiding in the low-light corners of a sedentary day—and widening your aperture lets the day back in.

Here's the wider frame.

Like a RAW file, our lives hold more dynamic range than we often let surface. This book isn't here to impose rules. It's here to widen the aperture, recover contrast, and help you recompose your days with a clearer frame.

Now, not later. The most important moment is the one you can act on.

Not because the world is loud—but because your quiet truth is finally ready to be lived. You don't need a bigger lens. Just the will to lift the one already in your hands.

I didn't know it then, but I was already standing in the hinge—caught between the world that raised me and the world I was now responsible for shaping. The blackout just forced me to see it.

So before another frame slips past unexamined . . .

Open your aperture. Let the light in. Step into focus. Begin.

Let's make this real for a moment.

An invitation: Three-Minute Frame Reset

1. Stand up.
2. Inhale for 4 counts, hold for 4, exhale for 6. Repeat three times.
3. Ask yourself: What's one thing I can observe—not fix—about my body or my mindset today? Write it down.

That's your first data point. Your first honest frame. And maybe, the first breath of a new healthspan.

The shutter slammed shut that day.
But in the darkness, my vision began to adapt.

CHAPTER 2

MOTION STEADIES THE "E" IN EMOTION

{ from dysregulation to rhythm }

I pressed the shutter in the parking lot after my mother's funeral—and the frame went black. Grief yanked the lens closed before I could even find my next breath.

Months later, when the world narrowed to the four walls of a cell, there was nowhere to run and everything to feel. If I couldn't move my body across distance, I learned to move my emotions through it: a deliberate stretch at dawn, a counted breath between hours, a sentence scrawled on scrap paper. Morning light rarely slipped through the bars, replaced instead by the steady hum of artificial light as I stretched the only way I could. My body moved an inch at a time, testing what still worked, what still hurt, what still held. It wasn't progress, but it was presence.

The blackout and the confinement taught the same lesson: Stillness can silence us unless we let feeling travel through the body and back into motion.

The lesson deepened when the world narrowed even further.

When the heavy steel door clicked shut, my world shrank to a few square feet. I discovered that even the smallest shift in posture could change the signal in my brain. This was the first lesson of the blackout: *Motion steadies the "E" in Emotion.*

To understand why motion matters, we have to start earlier.

Here, I return to the first small movements that helped me find steadiness when the ground felt unsteady.

THE PRELUDE OF FEELING

MOTION AND EMOTION ARE NOT SEPARATE EVENTS; THEY ARE SIMPLY DIFFERENT EXPOSURES OF THE SAME FILM. Before we speak, we move. And long before we learn to regulate our feelings with language, we regulate them with our bodies. Emotion begins long before language. As infants, emotion and motion arrive in tandem—a cry for hunger flanked by flailing limbs. The energy of an unmet need instantly manifests as physical turbulence. This fundamental connection is hardwired into us. The feeling of being "out of control" is a physical feeling first, a psychological label second. When you can no longer manage the weight of the emotion, your body—your original regulator—is the first thing to stiffen, freeze, or recoil.

But aging brings nuance. Emotions diversify: joy gains edges, sadness folds into memory, anger softens with understanding. Our bodies grow disciplined, deliberate—and sometimes distant. The emotional palette grows faster than motion's capacity to express it. This is why we must begin by learning to manage the subtle bias that creeps into the emotional system: dysregulation.

Here's the tension most of us feel but rarely name.

WHAT HAPPENS WHEN OUR EMOTIONS OUTPACE OUR MOTIONS?

When the richness of inner feeling eclipses the body's ability to respond, we face a frontier—not a flaw. Inside the V.I.T.A.L. framework, this tension becomes instructive. It calls for agency, not apology. It reveals that honoring emotional truth is as vital as any motion we make.

A different lens helps us see this more clearly.

Emotion as Shutter Speed. If motion is the image, emotion is the shutter speed.

This metaphor invites us to consider exposure:
- Quick shutter speeds freeze sharp bursts—moments of instinct.
- Slower speeds blur into lingering emotions like grief or longing.

Emotion filters our experiences. It shapes what gets captured, how long it's felt, what gets lost in shadow or overexposed in light. Through this lens, motion becomes an extension of emotional readiness, not a separate act.

Just as a photographer chooses settings based on light and subject, we navigate our world through emotional filters—sometimes unconsciously. The challenge is learning to adjust the settings with intention. You've just adjusted the light in your mind's frame—now pause enough to really see what's there before the next movement begins. The shutter has clicked, and in that still frame your own eyes are the subject.

Now let's bring this into your own frame.

Question: *What do you feel when you meet your own eyes?*

Purpose: Hold your lens steady long enough to see beyond the surface—catching the quiet truths that shape your next movement.

Prompts:
- I begin most days with a clear idea of how I want to show up.
- My actions are generally aligned with my deeper values.
- I regularly create space for reflection and honest self-evaluation.

Micro-action:
Close your eyes for two breaths. Notice your shoulders—lift, roll back, let them settle. Listen for the faintest background sound—the hum of air, a ticking clock, a bird outside. Let that sound become your metronome as you open your eyes and write one word for what you feel.

Why it works:
- Anchors the reader in their body and gives a sensory cue (shoulders/breath) before a cognitive label.

What's happening inside us is also happening around us.

GLOBAL EMOTIONAL TRENDS

Here's why these numbers matter for daily life.

Global Emotional Instability and Contagion

Between 2008 and 2021, a *BMC Public Health* analysis of 2.4 million people across 149 countries found:
- 85% of nations report worsening emotional stress over time
- Young adults saw the fastest declines in well-being

- The COVID-19 pandemic accelerated instability in every living and working environment[9]

Emotional contagion research shows that negative feelings (fear, anger, anxiety) spread more rapidly than positive ones. In high-stress settings—workplaces, social media, political events—mirror-neuron activation makes us *literally* catch each other's mood, undermining trust and cooperation.[10]

Why it matters: As our world grows more emotionally charged, the V.I.T.A.L. pillars become not just self-help but social stabilization.

Emotional Contagion and Social Cohesion

- When we're surrounded by negativity, our own emotional regulation falters.
- Leaders and communities with high emotional intelligence can buffer contagion—but few have effective tools.
- V.I.T.A.L.'s "Values" and "Intentionality" pillars become anchors, filtering social noise through personal meaning and mindful choice.

9   Piao, Xiangdan, Jun Xie, and Shunsuke Managi. Continuous Worsening of Population Emotional Stress Globally: Universality and Variations. BMC Public Health 24, no. 3576 (December 2024). https://link.springer.com/article/10.1186/s12889-024-20961-4.

10   Lu, Dan, and Dian Hong. Emotional Contagion: Research on the Influencing Factors of Social Media Users' Negative Emotional Communication During the COVID-19 Pandemic. *Frontiers in Psychology* 13 (2022). https://doi.org/10.3389/fpsyg.2022.931835.

Think of emotional contagion as a ripple, not a reaction.

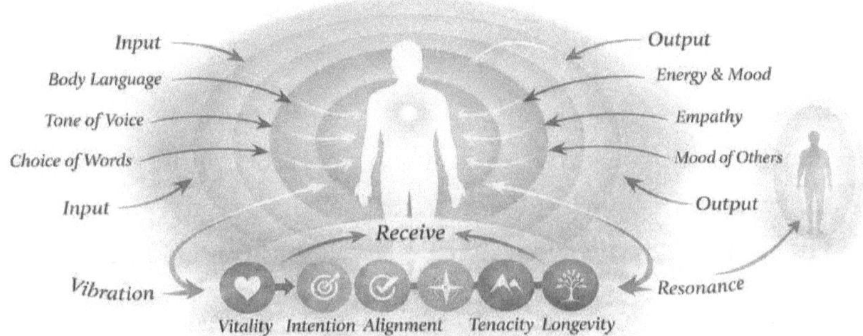

Emotions ripple outward like currents tugging at your footing. The next step you take decides whether you drift or steer. This moment is the rudder. The current tugs, and the horizon shifts in the viewfinder—choose whether to reframe or drift with it.

Before we explore tools for recovery, it helps to name what we're working with: Dysregulation is when the body's emotional response overwhelms its ability to return to baseline. In those moments, clarity blurs and direction feels lost. That's why the first Shutter Speed Check—Alignment and Direction—matters. Just as a camera's shutter speed can steady an image, pausing to notice alignment helps us recalibrate when emotions run ahead of our capacity to recover. This is not about perfection but presence: slowing down enough to restore coherence, reclaim agency, and move forward with dignity.

> *Motion regulates emotion. Emotion shapes motion.*
> *Healthspan grows at their intersection.*

Question: *Do you move from survival, habit, or intention?*

Purpose: Sharpen the "why" behind your actions so they don't get blurred by someone else's focus.

Prompts:
- I keep my routines alive even when they feel uphill.
- I meet setbacks with reflection, not self-judgment.
- I'm consistent with what matters, even without an audience.

Micro-action:
Stand and take one slow step forward, as if into your next choice. Feel which part of your foot lands first—heel, ball, or toe—and jot the word "survival," "habit," or "intention" beside it.

Why it works:
The physical cue becomes a metaphor they'll remember next time they step into a tense situation.

EMOTIONAL ARCHITECTURE OF V.I.T.A.L.

Emotion is the cornerstone of each pillar. Here's how it threads through the framework:

Pillar	Emotional Drivers	Emotional Focus	Guiding Question
Vitality	Awe, joy, curiosity—feelings that energize the pursuit of meaningful aging	Energy & Aliveness	Where is my spark fading or shining?
Intention	Dignity, empathy, self-respect—core emotions that root values and conscious action	Purpose & Direction	Why am I choosing this movement now?

Pillar	Emotional Drivers	Emotional Focus	Guiding Question
Tenacity	Anticipation, patience, readiness—emotions that shape when and how we move	Quiet Resilience & Commitment	What keeps me showing up when it's hard?
Alignment	Fear, trust, wonder—dynamic emotions that signal when to bend, stretch, or stand firm	Presence & Coherence	Is my effort in sync with my values?
Longevity	Nostalgia, reverence, gratitude—sentiments that tether us to generational resilience	Endurance & Legacy	What impact do I want to leave behind?

WHY THESE PILLARS MATTER TODAY

From feeling to motion. Emotion begins the story, but motion finishes the sentence.

As the emotional landscape shifts, our physical selves follow—sometimes with precision, sometimes reluctantly. Yet motion remains a powerful interpreter. It mirrors the emotion within, whether in posture, pace, or pause.

In aging, we face moments where emotion surges while the body slows. But this is not an undoing—it's an invitation. To adapt. To be deliberate. To choose movement that honors what we feel, even if it's less pronounced than before.

Inside V.I.T.A.L., emotion is the unseen guide. And motion, when shaped by dignity and agency, becomes not just possible—but purposeful.

THE EMOTIONAL PILLAR OF V.I.T.A.L.: ALIGNMENT

Why Alignment?

Alignment is the pillar of coherence—the place where emotion, values, and action converge.

- When your external motion reflects your internal truth, emotion flows freely.
- When misaligned, emotion becomes resistance: frustration, fatigue, unease.
- When aligned, emotion becomes flow: calm, clarity, integrity, even joy.

How each pillar touches emotion:

Pillar	Emotional Role
Vitality	Emotion as fuel or depletion (energy states: joy, exhaustion, excitement, apathy)
Intention	Emotion as motive (desire, love, grief, curiosity)
Tenacity	Emotion as endurance (resilience through fear, disappointment, or self-doubt)
Alignment	Emotion as feedback (truth, peace, integrity, friction)
Longevity	Emotion as memory (gratitude, regret, legacy, continuity)

When your values and actions meet cleanly, grace steadies the waters. Step into this moment as if the moon itself has lined up with your tide, and consider how every encounter could open and close on that same light. When the moon of your values aligns with the tide of your actions, the waters flow steady and clear. Grace isn't passive—it's the gentle turn of the tide that carries both vessels to shore.

--- Shutter Speed Check—Transformation Through Grace

Question:
How would grace change this encounter?

Purpose:
Let the emotional tide carry into the shoreline of action—so dignity travels with you.

Prompts:
- I pause before answering in tense moments.
- I find one constructive element in every exchange.
- I close conversations in a way that leaves dignity intact.

Micro-action:
Before moving on, think of one conversation today. In your notes, write a one-line opening and closing you could use that would leave both people's dignity intact.

Why it works:
Grace becomes tangible; we practice language before the real moment arrives.

Alignment is where emotion and intention meet in motion.

Shutter Question	Which emotion is guiding me now—and does it fit who I want to be?
Metaphor	Alignment is the emotional tide When the moon of your values aligns with the ocean of your actions, the tide flows strong and clean. When misaligned, it churns into chaos.
Emotional Feedback	• If your emotion doesn't match your movement, check alignment. • Do your choices resonate or resist your deeper values? • Are you acting out of fear, duty, joy, or hope?

Sometimes clarity comes not from adding more light but by removing what distracts from the subject. Strip back the frame so only what matters remains in view. Sometimes power is what remains after the noise is gone. Clearing the shot sharpens the subject—and your next move. Like turning the focus ring until the subject snaps sharp, clarity comes when distractions fall away. With the frame cleared, the focal point stands out. Naming today's pillar is like choosing a focal point—everything else softens into the background.

--- Shutter Speed Check—Minimalism and Power

Question:
How am I moving through my world today?

Purpose:
Strip away visual and emotional clutter so your movement matches what matters.

Prompts:
- I choose actions that serve both my values and my energy.
- I simplify routines to remove nonessential friction.
- I notice where I can do less but better.

Micro-action:
Look around your current space. Remove one object from your visual field that doesn't serve this moment. Note how your breath or shoulders change.

Why it works:
Immediate cause and effect between environment and emotional load.

I pause in the hallway of my own day—between what I've chosen to release and what I still carry. The light feels different now, sharper against the pared-back frame. I notice the weight in my hand is less, yet the choice of what to hold next feels heavier.

Each day, one pillar quietly does the heavy lifting. Naming it is like locking focus—it sharpens every movement you make for the rest of the frame. Like a photographer choosing a single focal point, naming today's pillar lets everything else fall softly out of frame. With your hands on the camera, today's chosen pillar becomes the anchor point—the rest can drift softly out of frame.

Question:
Which pillar carries me most today?

Purpose:
Makes the framework a living companion—turning pillars from ideas into daily anchors.

Prompts:
- I can name the pillar most present in my decisions today.
- I notice when I'm leaning too heavily on one pillar.
- I choose one pillar to strengthen in this season.

Micro-action:
Circle the pillar you named. Put a star next to one action you'll take this week to strengthen it—something small enough to complete in under ten minutes.

Why it works:
Turns abstract pillar-naming into a commitment without overwhelming scope.

WHAT IT ALL MEANS

You are not simply living—you are moving, feeling, seeing, and becoming in ways shaped by your past, grounded in your present, and aimed toward a future of your own making.

The V.I.T.A.L. pillars are more than concepts; they are the way you translate emotion into motion and motion into a life that feels wholly yours. They help you feel what's real, move with purpose, and see with perspective. Through them, you stop reacting to life and start coauthoring it. Even grief can guide. Stillness can be a choice. Aging can be a practice.

You were given a body. You were given a lens. You were given love. And now, you are choosing how to move through the world with all of it.

Pillar	Means ...	Mantra
Vitality	You matter enough to recharge. Listen to your energy. Rest when you need it. Move not to burn out but to stay alive inside and out.	*"I check my battery, not just my to-do list."*
Intention	You choose why you move. Walk into a room with purpose. Eat, train, and speak with meaning.	*"I move toward what matters, not away from what hurts."*
Tenacity	You keep going—especially on hard days. Show up even when nobody claps.	*"I'm not where I want to be yet, but I haven't stopped showing up."*
Alignment	You live in sync with your body, values, and voice. Notice when something feels off and adjust.	*"What I do now feels like me."*
Longevity	You're in this for the long run. Move today so tomorrow still feels like yours.	*"I move today so that tomorrow still feels like mine."*

FRAMING YOUR NEXT SHOT

Emotion opens the aperture. Now we step through.

Before we enter movement fully, it's worth grounding what emotion asks of us.

Movement restores rhythm—physiologically and emotionally—when things feel out of control.

Next we explore motion as a language—how the ways we move across occupations, cultures, and life stages carry stories of resilience, adaptability, and intention.

We'll look at how motion stabilizes, expresses, and ultimately transforms emotion and how aging invites us to see movement as both narrative and strategy.

In the still frame you've just composed, the subject is you—but in the next, movement will speak for you. Every gesture, stride, and pause becomes a sentence in your ongoing story.

FROM CORE VALUES TO CORE MOVEMENT

In the first part of this journey, you named what truly matters and mapped the forces that shape how you live. Now those values begin to move.

The path ahead becomes your compass—linking mindset, movement, and meaning—so that every physical choice you make reflects the life you're intentionally building.

V.I.T.A.L. Pillar	Core Idea	Movement Pillar	How They Form a Living Feedback Loop
Vitality	Energy, rhythm, breath, recovery	Cardio	Cardiovascular training builds stamina and breath capacity—fueling energy for life.
Intention	Focus, clarity, alignment with purpose	Balance	Balance practices demand focus and mindfulness, mirroring intentional living.
Tenacity	Persistence, resilience, grit	Strength	Strength training requires discipline and repeated effort, embodying resilience.

V.I.T.A.L. Pillar	Core Idea	Movement Pillar	How They Form a Living Feedback Loop
Alignment	Integrity, posture, structural harmony	Mobility	Mobility work ensures joints and movement patterns are aligned and functional.
Longevity	Sustaining healthspan, graceful aging	Flexibility	Flexibility preserves movement over time, supporting lifelong adaptability.

Emotion opens the aperture, but what we step into next is just as important. Awareness alone can't steady us; it needs a structure—a way of moving through the world with clarity and intention.

That is the movement mindset at the heart of V.I.T.A.L.: a framework that turns feeling into motion, motion into meaning, and meaning into a life aligned with what truly matters.

Pause here if you need to.

MOVEMENT MINDSET

{ from resistance to rhythm }

In the blackout I learned something simple and stubborn: Movement begins long before the body follows. Each step down that hospital hallway was more than a physical act—it was a negotiation between fear and faith. I didn't merely move; I chose to move.

Months later, when confinement erased distance, that choice mattered even more. The negotiation didn't stop because the ground did. It shifted inward: posture, breath, the smallest deliberate gesture became the way I crossed a room I could not leave.

If I couldn't move my body across ground, I learned to move my emotions through my body. Breath steadied the signal. Posture reset the frame. A tiny, intentional motion became the pilot when everything else felt out of control. Mindset was not a passenger; it was the hand on the wheel.

The next lesson arrived quietly, in the space between motion and meaning.

This chapter explores the shift from reacting to choosing—the earliest signs of agency returning.

But emotion alone isn't enough. The mindset behind it matters just as much.

The blackout and the months that followed—when I was confined and forced to reckon with limits—made one thing clear: Movement begins long before the body follows. Each step down that hospital hallway, each small choice in a cell, was a negotiation between fear and faith. I didn't just move—I chose to. Mindset wasn't a passenger; it was the pilot.

In the first part of this journey, you named what truly matters and mapped the forces that shape how you live. Now those values begin to move.

Values are no longer ideas you carry in your mind; they become directions expressed through your body—through breath, posture, effort, and ease.

The path ahead becomes your compass—linking mindset, movement, and meaning—so that every physical choice you make reflects the life you're intentionally building.

Here's where the frame widens.

— | —

MOVEMENT, MINDSET, AND METRICS: THE V.I.T.A.L. BLUEPRINT

Every great photograph begins with three elements: subject, intention, and exposure. In your life's portrait, those correspond to Movement, Mindset, and Metrics. Each lens brings clarity to your vitality—your body in motion, your mind engaged, your progress illuminated.

Movement mindset is not about intensity—it's about identity. How we move shapes how we feel, decide, and age. If chapter 2 was about motion as regulation, this chapter is about movement as practice—a way of living on purpose.

Like photography, practice is not instantaneous—it is developed. The negative must be immersed, exposed, and patiently revealed before the image comes into focus. In the same way, movement as practice requires repetition, patience, and intention. Each step, stretch, or breath is a frame in the gallery of your life, slowly clarifying who you are becoming.

Let's frame this chapter as your working light meter: Learn how to compose each shot, develop the image, and build a living gallery of health, purpose, and legacy.

○
MOVEMENT DOMAINS:
COMPOSING THE PHYSICAL FRAME

Movement is your most powerful creative tool; it sculpts strength, resilience, and longevity. To build a V.I.T.A.L. practice, we train across five domains: Strength, Cardio, Flexibility, Mobility, and Balance. Each one supports emotional regulation, physical resilience, and long-term vitality.

Foundational Motion

- Why it matters: Adults who get at least 150 minutes of moderate activity weekly cut their risk of chronic disease and maintain independence into old age.

What to do:
- Break the total volume into 10-minute "movement snacks" between work tasks.
- Aim for 8,000–10,000 steps/day, then increase by 500 steps every two weeks.

Foundational motion is more than physical activity—it is the rhythm that carries us forward. To age with vitality, we must not only move but align our movement with intention, resilience, and renewal. The following V.I.T.A.L. Aging Movement Pillars illustrate how these forces come together, guiding us toward a life of agency, dignity, and hope.

To make this practical, we need a clearer map.

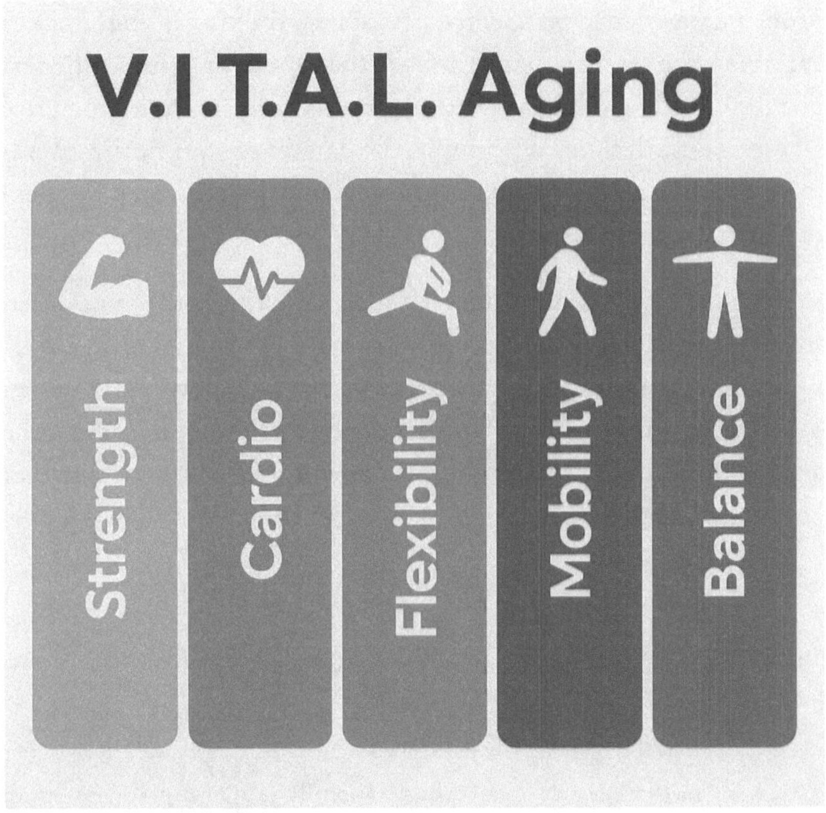

If you're reading this during your own narrowing, this is where momentum begins again.

Think of resistance training as both a lens and a dataset. A photographer adjusts focus to bring clarity to a subject. In the same way, strength work sharpens the body's definition. It preserves muscle mass that would otherwise blur with time. Each rep is like capturing light. One exposure may seem small, but together they build a vivid portfolio of resilience.

From a data science perspective, resistance training is your anchor variable—the feature that stabilizes the model of aging. It boosts metabolic rate, reduces all-cause mortality, and acts as a protective factor against decline. Without it, the dataset of your health trends toward noise and loss; with it, the signal remains strong and predictive of vitality.

In aging, strength is not vanity—it is structure. It is the tripod that steadies the camera, the algorithm that keeps the model accurate. By training your muscles, you preserve not only power and movement but also the dignity of independence. Resistance training is the anchor point in the scatterplot of longevity, the through line that keeps your story in focus.

STRENGTH REFLECTION

Strength is more than force—it's the quiet capacity to hold, lift, and carry what matters.

Before you enter the Lens Check, pause here.

What have you carried lately—physically, emotionally, relationally? Where do you feel strong, and where do you feel tender?

Strength is not just about effort—it's about endurance with grace.

Three planes—sagittal, frontal, transverse—keep your shot from toppling.

Drills: Squat to press; lateral lunge with reach; lunge with torso twist.

Quick Win: Train one underused plane this week.

○

MOVEMENT DOMAIN: STRENGTH—QUICK PRESCRIPTION

Why It Matters	Resistance training preserves muscle mass, boosts metabolic rate, and reduces all-cause mortality. It's your anchor in aging.
Metaphor	Strength is your tripod—it stabilizes the lens so clarity can emerge.
Key Actions	2–3 compound moves (e.g., squats, deadlifts, push-ups), 3 sets of 8–12 reps.
Quick Win	Add one extra rep to your next push-up or plank set.
Micro-Practice	Chair Stand Test • Sit in a chair, feet flat, arms crossed over chest. • Stand up and sit down 5–10 times without using your hands. • Notice stability, fatigue, and breath. Why: Builds lower-body strength and shows baseline resilience.

Cardiovascular training is like keeping your camera's shutter open long enough to capture the full sweep of light—it sustains the exposure that brings clarity to the image. Each session strengthens the heart's rhythm, much like a steady tripod prevents blur. The result is sharper focus not only in the body but in the mind and emotions as well.

From a data science perspective, cardio is your system's uptime. It keeps the model running and processing inputs. It delivers reliable outputs. Without it, the system risks downtime—missed signals, gaps in performance, and degraded accuracy. With it, your life's dataset stays continuous, resilient, and rich with usable information.

Cardio doesn't just extend life; it enhances the quality of each frame and each data point. It improves heart health, builds emotional resilience, and sharpens cognitive clarity. It is the ongoing calibration that keeps the lens clean and the algorithm stable, ensuring that your story is captured with vitality and precision.

CARDIO REFLECTION

Cardio is rhythm, breath, and persistence. It's the pulse of your story in motion.

Take a moment.

What gets your heart moving—literally and metaphorically? Where do you feel winded, and where do you feel energized?

Cardio reminds us: Movement is life, and rhythm is resilience.

Fast shutters freeze action; slow shutters reveal the flow.

Micro-Act: After a charged moment, take a 10-minute brisk walk and notice recovery time.

Why It Works: Adjusting pace teaches your system when to surge and when to rest.

○

MOVEMENT DOMAIN: CARDIO—QUICK PRESCRIPTION

Why It Matters	Cardiovascular training improves heart health, emotional resilience, and cognitive clarity. It's your system's uptime.
Metaphor	Cardio is your shutter speed—it captures your motion of life's light.
Key Actions	Moderate intensity: 150 minutes/week. High intensity: 75 minutes/week.
Quick Win	Take a 10-minute walk after your next emotionally charged moment.
Micro-Practice	3-Minute Pulse Walk • Walk briskly for 3 minutes. • Take your pulse before and 1 minute after. • Track how quickly your heart rate recovers. Why: Even a short burst teaches awareness of heart health and recovery.

Flexibility is your aperture—the opening that determines how much light you let in. A narrow aperture sharpens the world, bringing more of the scene into focus. A wider one softens the edges, isolating what matters most, inviting possibility and life. Flexibility protects your joints. It prevents falls. It supports graceful aging by keeping your body open to movement instead of closed by stiffness.

From a data science perspective, flexibility is like increasing the dimensionality of your dataset. The more features you can access, the richer the model becomes. When your range of motion is limited, the dataset shrinks, and the model struggles to adapt. But when you maintain flexibility, you preserve optionality—the ability to respond to new inputs, to adjust to unexpected variables, to keep the system resilient.

Flexibility is not about contortion or extremes; it's about adaptability. It's the aperture that widens your capacity to engage with life and the dataset that ensures your system can keep learning. By tending to flexibility, you give yourself the dignity of graceful movement, the agency to recover from imbalance, and the hope of continuing to open—to light, to possibility, to life itself.

FLEXIBILITY REFLECTION

Flexibility is the art of adaptation. It's the grace to bend, stretch, and respond to change.

Pause here.

Where have you stretched recently—physically, emotionally, or relationally? What helps you stay open when life shifts?

Flexibility is not weakness—it's wisdom in motion.

The wider the opening, the more light—and possibility—floods in.

Micro-Act: Morning reach + gentle forward fold before the day begins.

Why It Works: Keeps joints ready to "let the light in" without strain.

○ MOVEMENT DOMAIN: FLEXIBILITY—QUICK PRESCRIPTION

Why It Matters	Flexibility protects joints, prevents falls, and supports graceful aging. It keeps your body moving with ease and reduces the strain of daily life.
Metaphor	Flexibility is your aperture—the opening that lets more light into your life.
Key Actions	Dynamic warm-ups, static cooldowns, foam rolling.
Quick Win	Hold a gentle stretch for 30 seconds while breathing slowly.
Micro-Practice	Morning Reach • Upon waking, stand tall, raise arms overhead, and reach side to side for 30–60 seconds. • Add gentle forward fold, letting arms dangle. Why: Restores length after sleep and prevents stiffness before the day begins.

As physical therapist Amy Cassady reminds us, even simple home exercises can curb stiffness and reduce fall risk—a reminder that flexibility is less about extremes and more about everyday adaptability.

Mobility is your lens calibration—the fine adjustment that determines how clearly you can respond to change. Just as a photographer dials in focus to capture shifting light or a moving subject, mobility allows you to adapt smoothly to life's transitions. Without calibration, even the best camera produces blurred images; without mobility, even strong muscles and steady endurance can falter when life demands a sudden shift.

From a data science perspective, mobility is the system's adaptability—the ability of a model to generalize when new variables appear. A rigid model clings to the past and falters when conditions shift. Likewise, a rigid body resists the unexpected—a sudden turn, a stumble, a new demand. Mobility expands the range of possible responses, ensuring the system remains resilient and accurate in real time.

Mobility protects joints, prevents falls, and sustains independence. It is the quiet skill that keeps the picture sharp and the dataset relevant. By tending to mobility, you preserve not only freedom of movement but also the dignity of being able to meet change with clarity, balance, and grace.

MOBILITY REFLECTION

Mobility is freedom. It's the ability to move through space, time, and transition with ease.

Before the Lens Check, reflect:

Where do you feel fluid and free? Where do you feel stuck or limited?

Mobility invites you to reclaim motion—not just in body but in mindset.

Smoothly shifting from one subject to another keeps the story sharp.

Drills: Joint circles, cat-cow; lunge-to-twist flow.

Quick Win: 3 minutes of joint rotations before bed to recalibrate for tomorrow.

○

MOVEMENT DOMAIN: MOBILITY—QUICK PRESCRIPTION

Why It Matters	Mobility is the ability to move freely through full range. It's your lens calibration—how clearly you respond to change.
Metaphor	Mobility is your autofocus—it adjusts to shifting conditions.
Key Actions	Multi-planar drills. Joint articulation. Flow sequences.
Quick Win	Do 3 minutes of joint rotations before bed
Micro-Practice	Joint Circles • Slowly circle ankles, wrists, shoulders, and hips 5–10 times each direction. • Move smoothly, no rush, noticing range of motion. Why: Lubricates joints, reduces stiffness, supports daily adaptability.

Balance is your internal gyroscope—the quiet stabilizer that keeps you upright when the world shifts. In photography, balance is what keeps the frame from tilting, the horizon from slipping off center. A well-balanced composition draws the eye with ease; without it, even the sharpest image feels unsettled. In the body, balance prevents injury, sharpens proprioception, and supports emotional steadiness, giving you the confidence to move through life without fear of falling.

From a data science perspective, balance is the normalization step—the process that ensures no single variable overwhelms the model. Without it, the system skews, predictions falter, and outcomes lose reliability. With balance, the dataset remains stable, adaptable, and trustworthy, even when new inputs arrive.

Balance is not static. It's dynamic calibration. It's the tripod that steadies the camera in shifting light. It's also the algorithm that keeps the model from drifting off course. By cultivating balance, you preserve independence, protect your body, and nurture the emotional steadiness that allows you to meet change with clarity and grace.

BALANCE REFLECTION

Balance is the quiet coordination of opposites. It's the dance between effort and ease, strength and surrender.

Take a breath.

Where in your life do you feel steady? Where do you wobble, and what helps you recover?

Balance isn't static—it's responsive. Let's honor your rhythm.

Even on uneven ground, you can keep the shot true.

Micro-Act: Single-leg stand while brushing teeth; eyes closed for added challenge.

Why It Works: Stability under wobble keeps the composition intact.

O

MOVEMENT DOMAIN: BALANCE—QUICK PRESCRIPTION

Why It Matters	Balance prevents injury, sharpens proprioception, and supports emotional steadiness. It's your internal gyroscope.
Metaphor	Balance is your horizon line—it keeps your frame level when life tilts.
Key Actions	Static drills. Dynamic drills. Integrated balance.
Quick Win	Stand on one leg while brushing your teeth. Track your breath and thoughts as you stabilize.
Micro-Practice	Single-Leg Stand • Stand on one leg for up to 30 seconds, then switch. • For more challenges: close eyes or stand on a softer surface. Why: Trains stability and fall prevention, critical for long-term independence.

PUTTING IT ALL TOGETHER

Each movement domain carries its own emotional signature—and, like a photographer adjusting settings, each shapes the way you capture life in motion. Strength is your tripod: It anchors the frame so everything else holds steady. Cardio sets your exposure time—finding the tempo of pace and recovery that gives your days clarity without blur. Flexibility is your wide aperture, opening you to more light, more range, more possibility. Mobility turns the focus ring, letting you shift smoothly from one posture, task, or season to the next without losing sharpness. And Balance is your horizon line, the quiet calibration that keeps the shot level no matter how uneven the ground beneath you. Together, they're not just physical skills—they're how you compose the living image of yourself.

In Simple Terms: The Five Movement Domains

Each domain is like a setting on your life's camera. Strength steadies the frame. Cardio sets the rhythm. Flexibility widens the view. Mobility keeps the focus sharp. Balance levels the shot. Together, they don't just keep you moving—they help you move through life with confidence, clarity, and grace.

Strength	This is your muscle power. It's what lets you lift groceries, climb stairs, or carry your grandchild without strain. A little resistance training now means more independence later.
Cardio	This is your heart and lungs at work. It's the walk that clears your head, the bike ride that steadies your mood, the game that leaves you smiling and sweaty. Cardio keeps your system humming.
Flexibility	This is your ability to bend and reach. It's tying your shoes without wincing, stretching for the top shelf, or rolling out of bed without stiffness. Flexibility keeps you open to life's movements.

Mobility	This is your freedom to move smoothly. It's turning to check traffic, stepping off a curb, or twisting to grab something from the back seat. Mobility is what makes strength and cardio usable in real life.
Balance	This is your steady footing. It's standing on one leg to put on socks, walking across uneven ground, or catching yourself before a stumble. Balance is quiet confidence in motion.

As you move through these domains, ask yourself:
Which one am I leaning on today?
Which one is asking for attention?
THERE'S NO NEED TO
ANSWER PERFECTLY—ONLY HONESTLY.
If you want the full resources—assessment tables, synergy patterns,
and micro-drills—those live in the appendices, ready when you are.

MOVEMENT: ACTIVE RECOVERY

Covers restorative movement strategies, mobility work, and low-intensity activity that supports long-term performance and resilience.

MINDFUL MOVEMENT AND BREATH

Integrating awareness and breath turns exercise into a nervous-system tune-up.

- Practice: 4-count inhale, 6-count exhale during bodyweight sets.
- Why it matters: Slow diaphragmatic breathing activates your parasympathetic "rest and digest" system—lowering cortisol, enhancing recovery, and sharpening focus.

STRATEGIC RECOVERY

Your body builds strength during rest—sleep and active recovery are your darkroom process.

- Sleep hygiene: blackout curtains, no screens after 9 p.m., consistent wake time.
- Active recovery: light cycling, yoga, or a 10–20 minute nap flush metabolic "fog."
- Evidence: Sleep extension and strategic napping consistently boost both physical and cognitive performance in athletes.

Your mindset frames every choice—growth-oriented thinking transforms setbacks into brilliant exposures.

Growth Mindset: Developing Film Positively

- Core idea: Feedback is data, not judgment.
- Practice: After each session, journal one win, one challenge, one tweak.
- Impact: Small adjustments compound into lasting habits.

Reflective Journaling and Visualization

- "Contact sheet" review: Bullet-journal your triumphs, tensions, and tomorrow's micro-goals.
- Mental rehearsal: Preview your next workout or shoot in vivid detail—neural priming that improves execution.

Narrative Identity and Purpose

- Anchor question: "Whose story am I telling today?"
- Action: Before each session, remind yourself "I train to honor [mentor/parent/future self]."

Data are not cold—they're the invisible threads tying habits to outcomes.

Physical Performance Metrics

- Key metrics: weekly mileage, strength volume (weight × reps), plank or dead-hang duration.
- Monthly check: Is volume up by 5–10 percent? If not, adjust pace (shutter speed) or load (aperture).

Biometric and Recovery Data

- Tools: HRV, resting heart rate, sleep-tracker outputs.
- Interpretation: Rising HRV + stable/↓ RHR = ready to push. Falling HRV + ↑ RHR = schedule extra recovery.

Cognitive and Emotional Indicators

- Logs: rate mood/focus on a 1–5 scale.
- Cross-reference: Blue-hour dips often signal a need for a nap or extra stretch.

Dashboarding and Storyboarding

- Blend: Analog bullet-journal spreads + digital wearable summaries.
- Gallery view: Spot plateaus before they become burnout and breakthroughs that deserve celebration.

BRINGING IT ALL TOGETHER

By weaving Movement (science-backed routines), Mindset (growth thinking), and Metrics (data-driven insight), you create a living V.I.T.A.L. framework:

1. Move with intention—simple steps, progressive loads, deliberate recovery.
2. Think like an artist—interpret feedback, rehearse success, anchor purpose.
3. Measure intelligently—use data as insight, not judgment.

Next assignment: Pick one goal (e.g., add 10 seconds to dead-hang time), apply all three lenses for one week, then journal and compare. When you revisit this chapter, your gallery will show growth in vivid color—a legacy taking shape one frame, one breath, one data point at a time.

Numbers can inform us, but they can't define us. The value of any metric depends on the awareness behind it—not the precision of the data itself.

Metrics are how we frame progress—but every frame limits the field of view.

Data can show trends, but it can't capture the quality of a moment, the grace in persistence, or the small victories that don't register on a chart. As you move into V.I.T.A.L. in Action, think of these scores not as grades but as reflections—snapshots that reveal where you're aligned and where you might need to refocus. What matters most isn't the number but the noticing.

V.I.T.A.L. IN ACTION

Here's a simple, subjective 1–10 system you can apply to any activity—whether it's barre, HIIT, pickleball, running, or yoga—to rate how much each session taxes or trains the five movement domains:

- 1–3 = minimal engagement
- 4–6 = moderate / maintenance level
- 7–9 = high / challenging
- 10 = maximal / near-limit effort

JUSTIFICATION OF V.I.T.A.L. SCORES

I learned to count my breath before I learned to count my reps. In a cell, a single balanced posture felt like a small victory. The Barre score below translates those tiny wins into usable data—less to judge yourself, more to notice change.

Below are the subjective 1–10 ratings for barre, pickleball, and swimming, with rationales grounded in movement demands and expert commentary.

Barre[11,12,13]

Domain	Score	Rationale
Strength	7	Repetitive isometric holds and small pulses under constant tension build significant muscular endurance and mid-range strength.
Cardio	4	Low-impact sequences keep heart rate modest; few jumps or high-intensity drills limit cardiovascular load.
Flexibility	8	Inspired by ballet and yoga, classes emphasize deep hip, spine, and shoulder openings through dynamic stretches and holds.
Mobility	7	Multi-planar transitions—pliés, relevés, foldovers—require joint articulation, especially in hips and ankles.
Balance	9	Continuous tiny movements at the barre and single-leg pulses demand precise core engagement and proprioception.

11   Waters, J. What Is Barre (and What Are the Benefits)? Cleveland Clinic Health, 2025.

12   Laroia, V. A Guide to Barre Terminology. VinitaYoga, 2023.

13   Falk, M. Barre Is the Trendy, Low-Impact Workout Your Routine Is Missing. Well+Good, 2024.

Pickleball[14]

Domain	Score	Rationale
Strength	5	Lunges, knee-drives, and quick volleys engage quads, glutes, and core, but loads remain moderate compared to heavy lifts.
Cardio	6	Up-and-back rallies and minimal rest between points yield intermittent, moderate-intensity bursts.
Flexibility	4	Occasional low digs and knee drives ask for hip and shoulder ROM, but overall range demands are modest.
Mobility	7	Split-steps, lateral shuffles, and rapid in-court adjustments drive agility and multi-directional joint flow.
Balance	8	A slightly forward, knees-bent ready stance and frequent weight-shifts on toe balls underpin strong court stability.

Swimming (Front Crawl)[15]

Domain	Score	Rationale
Strength	7	Propulsion relies on sustained upper-body pulls and core stabilization against water resistance.
Cardio	10	Continuous full-stroke laps demand near-maximal aerobic output over prolonged durations.
Flexibility	6	Efficient catch and pull phases require moderate shoulder and hip extension to optimize stroke length.
Mobility	7	Coordinated hip-hinge in kicks and full shoulder rotation for each arm cycle call for good joint mobility.
Balance	6	Maintaining a streamlined, horizontal body position in water demands steady core control and trim.

14   Parfait, Sid. Pickleball Movement and Balance. PickleTip.com, 2025.
15   Zamparo, Paolo, et al. Movement Evaluation of Front Crawl Swimming: Technical Skill versus Aesthetic Quality. PLOS ONE 12, no. 2 (2017): e0170670. https://pubmed.ncbi.nlm.nih.gov/28886063.

The practices outlined here are meant to spark reflection and agency. For those ready to put these ideas into motion, a collection of activity lists and a thirty-day renewal challenge can be found in Appendix A: Practice Companions. This section offers practical steps to embody the principles of renewal in daily life.

How to tailor this to you:
1. After each session, pause and ask yourself, "On a 1–10 scale, how much did I challenge my strength? Cardio . . . ?"
2. Track the scores for a week. Look for imbalances (e.g., low mobility vs. high cardio).
3. Adjust your plan—if flexibility sits at 3–4 across most workouts, add a dedicated stretch or long-exposure "slow shutter" flow.

Over time, you'll build a personalized "movement fingerprint" showing where you're strong and where you need more focus—and you'll bring true balance to your V.I.T.A.L. practice.

How to apply:
1. After each session, rate the five domains.
2. Track weekly averages to spot imbalances.
3. Adjust your plan—e.g., add mobility drills if your mobility scores stay low.

This simple schema lets you compare any activity and ensure holistic movement in your V.I.T.A.L. practice.

| KEY TAKEAWAYS:

- Strength runs from near zero (meditation) to max effort (powerlifting).
- Cardio spans barely any heart-rate rise (sitting) to all-out intervals (HIIT).
- Flexibility hits its low in rigid lifts and peaks in gymnastics.
- Mobility is minimal on a stationary bike but off the charts in parkour.

- Balance is trivial in the water yet paramount on a slackline.

Use this to spot gaps in your week: If flexibility stays in the 1–4 zone, add a longer yoga or gymnastics-style session; if balance never approaches 10, sneak in a few slacklining drills or single-leg stances.

Movement isn't just physical—it's emotional, relational, and spiritual. Appendix B offers a reflection to help you track your own movement domains. Use it to notice patterns, celebrate progress, and stay grounded in what restores you.

The Movement Domains are not the V.I.T.A.L. pillars—they are the raw signals from which your pillar patterns emerge.

FACTORS INFLUENCING YOUR V.I.T.A.L. SESSION SCORES

Different personal and external factors can skew your 1–10 ratings on strength, cardio, flexibility, mobility, and balance. Tracking these alongside your session helps you interpret trends more accurately.

Physiological Factors

- Age and Life Stage

Muscular power, recovery speed, and joint resilience naturally shift over decades, altering perceived effort and capacity.

- Body Battery / Energy Reserve

Metrics like "body battery," heart-rate variability, and resting heart rate reflect your available energy and stress load going into a workout.

- Sleep Quality and Duration

Poor or fragmented sleep raises perceived exertion, slows neuromuscular performance, and blunts flexibility.

- Nutrition and Hydration

Fuel timing, macronutrient balance, and fluid status directly impact endurance, strength output, and mobility.

- Recovery Status and Delayed-Onset Muscle Soreness (DOMS)
Residual muscle soreness or fatigue from prior sessions reduces both performance and how you perceive effort.

- Injury, Pain, and Joint Health
Acute aches or chronic conditions force compensations, lowering mobility/flexibility and sometimes strength.

Lifestyle and Environmental Factors

- Stress and Mental Fatigue
High cognitive or emotional stress makes sessions feel harder, particularly cardio and strength work.

- Time of Day and Circadian Rhythm
Peak strength, flexibility, and alertness vary—many athletes lift best in the late afternoon, but morning cardio can feel sluggish.

- Temperature, Humidity, and Altitude
Extreme heat and cold or thin air drive up heart rate and perceived difficulty, especially for cardio domains.

- Equipment & Facility Setup
Slippery floors, heavy bars, unfamiliar machines or cramped spaces can alter movement quality and balance demands.

Psychological and Technical Factors

- Motivation and Focus
A distracted mind or low motivation often down-rates every domain by increasing perceived effort.

- Technical Skill and Familiarity

Mastery of movement patterns (e.g., complex yoga flows or Olympic lifts) improves efficiency, boosting strength and mobility scores.

- Social Context and Coaching

Group energy, a motivating coach, or friendly competition can raise your output, particularly in cardio and strength.

Normalizing and Contextualizing Your Scores

- Log key factors (sleep hours, body battery, stress level, notes on pain) alongside your 1–10 ratings.
- Compare scores only against sessions under similar contexts (e.g., same time of day, recovery level).
- Apply adjustment weights—for instance, subtract 1–2 points on strength when body battery <20%, or add 0.5–1 point when well rested.
- Use rolling averages over 7–14 days to filter out one-off dips caused by travel, illness, or life-stress.

Beyond raw scores, consider layering in wearable insights—like heart-rate zones, sleep staging, or HRV trends—to deepen your V.I.T.A.L. practice and tailor each session to how your body truly feels.

Here's a concise mapping showing how our five V.I.T.A.L. pillars, their corresponding movement domains, core emotional "pillars," and photographic "sight" techniques all interlock:

Sight (Photography)	V.I.T.A.L. Pillar	Movement Pillar	Emotion Pillar
High-Key Exposure	Vitality	Cardio	Positive (joy/hope)
Selective Focus (shallow DoF)	Intention	Balance	Complex/Blended

Sight (Photography)	V.I.T.A.L. Pillar	Movement Pillar	Emotion Pillar
High-Contrast Black & White	Tenacity	Strength	Negative (anger/fear)
Leading Lines	Alignment	Mobility	Positive & Complex
HDR (Expanded Dynamic Range)	Longevity	Flexibility	Complex/Blended

How to read this:

- "Sight" names a photographic approach—how light, focus, contrast, lines, or range are rendered.
- Each sight parallels one V.I.T.A.L. pillar (Vitality, Intention, Tenacity, Alignment, Longevity).
- That pillar finds its physical expression in one movement domain (cardio, balance, strength, mobility, flexibility).
- And each also aligns with a dominant emotion type:
    - Positive (pure uplift)
    - Negative (challenge, grit)
    - Complex/Blended (nuanced, layered feelings)

Together they form an ecosystem:
- When you chase vitality you flood your system with cardio and positive emotion—like shooting a high-key frame.
- When you hone intention, you practice balance and hold a nuanced emotional focus—like dialing in a shallow depth of field.

. . . and so on.

And yet, practice remains possible. To move with identity is to reclaim motion as expression, to let the body catch up to the heart. Movement becomes not just a response but a choice—a way of living on purpose, even as the palette of feeling grows more complex.

This is the hinge the whole chapter turns on.

Once you understand how to relate to movement, the next step is learning how to measure what matters—without losing what's meaningful and without surrendering the agency that makes movement your own.

Every loop I was stuck in had been written long ago.
The screen dimmed, then flickered with possibility.

CHAPTER 4

MINDSET AND METRICS

{ calibrating your lens for a V.I.T.A.L. life }

As I walked those 13.1 miles, every image I made became a feedback loop—a test of clarity, pattern, and presence. Those hours were more than documentation; they were recalibration. The body steadied, the mind focused. Breath, pace, observation—simple tools that turned raw data into direction.

The blackout and the confinement had taught me to read the smallest signals: a tightened jaw, a shallow breath, a faltering step. In the field or in a cell, those signals are metrics. What we track, we begin to transform; what we measure, we learn to respect.

In these pages, I begin to understand how attention, data, and intention can work together to widen the frame again.

Now that we've explored motion and emotion, it's time to look at the signals beneath them.

Have you ever stood at the edge of a moment—sore, reflective, maybe even a little defeated—and realized that your tools, whether a camera, a code editor, or a yoga mat, are shaping how you grow?

Metrics are not just numbers; they are exposures in the portrait of your life. They reveal patterns, progress, and possibilities—but only if they remain tethered to meaning. Just as a light meter guides a photographer toward balance, the right measures guide you toward vitality without reducing your identity to data points.

I had one of those moments in the first week of summer 2025. It was a whirlwind: I survived one of the hardest ab routines in Sharon's classical barre class—led by a retired ballerina with no mercy—then got soundly beat in two rounds of singles pickleball. Still sweaty from the courts and craving solitude, I grabbed my camera and found myself on a quiet shoreline at Old Dominion University, chasing a sunset.

The sun broke over the horizon in golds and pinks, casting a path across the water—an everyday miracle, but one I could appreciate fully only when looking through the lens. In that moment of stillness, I realized how deeply photography and software engineering have shaped my life. Both require noticing patterns, respecting light—whether photons or data streams—and patiently waiting for the decisive moment. These actions, unknown to me, would plant the seed for V.I.T.A.L.—a framework for intentional aging grounded in practice, not just philosophy.

This isn't a manifesto—it's a practice, shaped by years of hands-on experience as a photographer and developer on the path from software engineering toward data engineering. In one of my development journal entries (June 12, 2018), I began a seven-day Kaggle course on Python scripting—a spark that ignited my curiosity in the world of data science. Nearly six years later, on March 9, 2024, I was measuring heart rate variability while combing through inefficient SQL plans—finding the bottlenecks in both code and cardio. Different domain, same mindset: monitor, reflect, iterate.

That moment taught me something numbers often reveal before we do.

Over the next chapters, I'll introduce you to V.I.T.A.L., a five-part framework for aging well—intellectually, emotionally, and physically:

- Vitality is about where to focus your energy. Like composing a photo, it's knowing what to sharpen and what to let blur.
- Intention bridges story and data—journals, dashboards, and how you track what matters.
- Tenacity explores tools that help you stick with hard things—from AI copilots to routines that support mobility, mood, and strength over time.
- Alignment is choosing the right challenges at the right time, whether it's crow pose, doing squats on an inverted Bosu ball, or refining a data model.
- Longevity ties it all together: the images, the code commits, the memories that whisper, "This mattered."

Think of this section—*Mindset and Metrics*—as your starter kit: a Rolleiflex for emotion, a notebook for your internal GPS, a script or two to measure growth, and a circle of fellow travelers walking the same path.

Before going further, take a breath and notice your body in this moment.

No framework lands in the mind alone; understanding comes through the posture, the breath, the small shifts of attention.

The ideas here aren't meant to be mastered all at once. Let them settle the way a photograph settles into clarity—slowly, quietly, in its own time.

In Simple Terms: Mindset	
Your mindset is the story you tell yourself. It's the frame you put around every experience.	
Growth Mindset	See feedback as information, not judgment. A stumble isn't failure—it's data you can use.
Reflection	Take a moment to notice what went well, what felt hard, and what you'd tweak next time.
Purpose	Remind yourself who or what you're showing up for. It could be your future self, a loved one, or simply the joy of progress.
Mindset is how you talk to yourself when no one else is listening. Keep the voice kind, curious, and forward-looking.	

Metrics aren't judgments—they're mirrors.

In Simple Terms: Metrics	
Metrics are just your way of keeping score—not to judge but to notice patterns.	
Performance Metrics	Track the basics: how far you walked, how many reps you lifted, how long you held a plank.
Recovery Metrics	Pay attention to sleep, heart rate, or just how rested you feel when you wake up.
Mood & Focus	Jot down a quick 1–5 rating for energy or clarity. It's as important as the numbers on your watch.
Metrics are your feedback loop. They help you see what's working, what's not, and where to adjust—like checking the light meter before you take the shot.	

By the end of this chapter, you won't just know what V.I.T.A.L. stands for—you'll have the gear, exercises, and reflective prompts to make it your own.

Aperture wide open. Focus locked. Data streaming. Let's begin.

Mindset and metrics work together—one gives meaning, the other gives direction.

Now that you can see your patterns, we can explore the five pillars that give those patterns shape.

Return to this section whenever the numbers feel louder than your life.

> *Too much light and we overexpose. Too much noise and we miss the signal. A moment of darkness.*

PART TWO

LIVING DELIBERATELY

CHAPTER 5

THE PILLARS OF V.I.T.A.L.

{ insights revealed through shadow }

For two days I kept my eyes closed—darkness felt safer than what light might demand. Then, on a Thursday evening, the dialysis room came into focus: faces, machines, gravity. Months later, in a cell no larger than a closet, that same scene translated into small, stubborn practices. From that room and that confinement a blueprint formed: Vitality, Intention, Tenacity, Alignment, Longevity.

If Part One helped you see more clearly, Part Two invites you to live more deliberately—at your own pace.

Here the framework comes into full view—not as a system to master but as a way of seeing your life with more clarity and steadiness.

Now that the ground is steady beneath us, it's time to name the pillars that hold the practice together.

If part one asked you to notice, part two invites you to build.

If the full toolbox feels like a lot, start small.

Here are three simple practices that take less than five minutes each and begin activating the pillars:

- One breath reset (Vitality)
- One intentional choice (Intention)
- One alignment check: "Is this action moving me closer to or further from what I value?"

This isn't a race. It's a rhythm. Begin where you are.

These pillars aren't theories—they're the patterns that emerged when I rebuilt my life from the inside out.

Brief Note Before the V.I.T.A.L. Framework

Before we step into the pillars, a quick pause. The V.I.T.A.L. framework grew out of lived experience, not theory. It isn't something to master— just a way of noticing your life with more clarity and intention. Move through the pillars at your own pace. Start where your season leads you. Let what resonates stay, and let the rest wait. This is a companion, not a prescription.

> ## HOW TO USE THE FRAMEWORK
>
> Start with the pillar that meets your season. Move at your own pace. Let one idea settle before reaching for the next. Return as needed. This framework is here to support your movement, not prescribe it.

THE V.I.T.A.L. FLOW

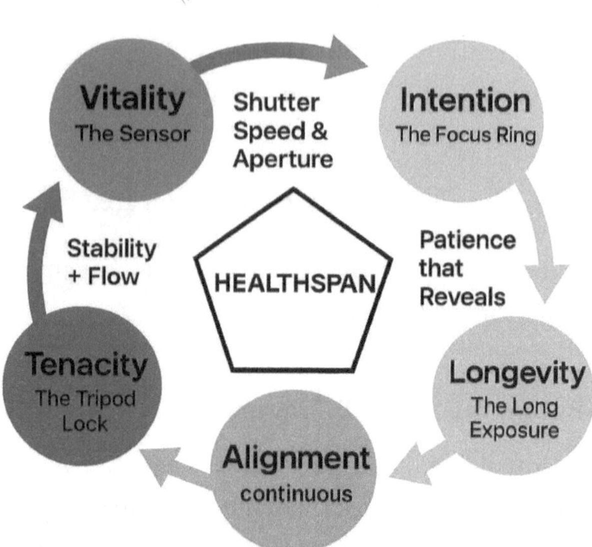

The V.I.T.A.L. Framework is a continuous-loop system. A deficiency in one area (e.g., Vitality) immediately compromises the function of the next (e.g. poor Intention). Prioritize continuous calibration.

This diagram offers a simple way to see where something in your life may be out of balance. Each pillar is expressed through a photography metaphor—a reminder that clarity comes from small adjustments in focus, light, and steadiness. Let it help you notice where you are and where a gentle recalibration might begin.

[V] VITALITY: ENERGY FOR LIFE

Here, we begin where all movement begins—with the kind of energy that rises not from force but from alignment.

Vitality depletes in many ways: The body grows heavy with fatigue, the mind dulls under stress, joy slips into indifference. These signals are not failures—they are feedback. They remind us that vitality must be renewed, not assumed.

Physical depletion shows up as muscle fatigue, sleep debt, or the dull ache of imbalance—the body whispering before it screams.

Emotional depletion arrives as discouragement after setbacks, stress that flattens joy, or the quiet erosion of motivation—the spirit dimming when purpose feels distant.

The shadow of Vitality is overstimulation—chasing energy without balance, mistaking constant motion for resilience. In this shadow, the body burns out and the spirit grows restless, reminding us that vitality is not about endless fuel but sustainable renewal.

I've seen both depletion and shadow in my own mornings. At 5:45 a.m., while most of the neighborhood still sleeps, I'm up. The rhythm of my routine is familiar now—warm-ups that wake not just my muscles but my mind. This isn't discipline born out of guilt or pressure. It's a conversation with my future self. A handshake with hope.

Vitality, for me, isn't about chasing youth. It's about honoring what's alive. It's about showing up to the body I've been given, whether it feels like a sports car or an old truck on any given day. I don't need to outrun age. I just need to move—fast enough to escape inertia, slow enough to avoid burnout.

When my Garmin watch said I hit a VO_2 max of forty-six at fifty-eight years old, I almost brushed it off. It wasn't a badge I sought out. But the numbers didn't lie—years of steady movement, consistent effort, and intentional rest had added up to something real. That stat told a deeper story: not of athleticism but of commitment. Of care. Of choosing to stay in the game.

The dead hangs, the fifty push-ups, the two-minute plank, the one-minute wall sit—they're benchmarks, yes. But they're also metaphors. They remind me that sometimes strength is hanging on. Sometimes it's enduring. And sometimes it's being still in discomfort without giving in to it.

I didn't always think this way. In my younger years, vitality was measured in extremes—in the rush of doing more, lifting heavier, proving something. Now, it's in the quiet consistency. The way I listen to my joints when they whisper before they scream. The way I recover not just with sleep but with presence. With walks. Breath. Reflection.

I think often about how vitality connects to legacy. I'm not training just for my own well-being. I want to be strong for my family, steady for my children, a living example of what endurance looks like when it's guided by purpose rather than ego. That's why I move. Why I lift. Why I pause and stretch when no one's watching.

Vitality is not reserved for the young—it belongs to the intentional. And as long as I wake up willing to meet the day with energy and care, I know I am still becoming. That's the quiet power behind all of this: the belief that we are not done. That our bodies are still worthy of our attention, not in spite of aging but because of it.

Vitality isn't about returning to our twenties. It's about reinhabiting our body with respect and joy. It's the capacity to engage with life—not for aesthetics but for connection. As we age, vitality allows us to stay curious, mobile, and alive to the world.

Vitality is the baseline hum of aliveness. Breath before movement. Readiness before effort. In data terms, it's your system's uptime—your ability to respond, recover, and stay operational when life surges.

You don't need to max out every day. But you do need to plug in. To recharge. To fuel. A brisk morning walk, a mindful breath, a stretch before the ache becomes chronic, a glass of water before the day accelerates—these are not indulgences. They are infrastructure.

Vitality gives us energy, but energy alone is not enough—it needs direction. That is where Intention begins.

VITALITY REFLECTION

Vitality is not just energy—it's engagement. It's the pulse of what makes you feel alive, connected, and responsive to the world around you.

Before you move into the Lens Questions, take a breath.

What activities, relationships, or environments restore your spark? Where do you feel most vibrant, and where do you feel most drained?

Vitality is not a fixed trait—it's a rhythm. Let's explore yours.

- Where in my daily rhythm do I allow true recovery?

- What "noise" is interfering with my body's energy signal?

- If my life were a photograph, would I need more light (energy) or less exposure (rest) to capture it clearly?

[•]   **Lens Check for Vitality *(ISO and Gentle Overexposure)***

Your ISO is your adaptability to light—or life. Small, chosen stressors sharpen your range.

Micro-Experiments: cold finish to a shower; short sauna sit; loaded carry; one-leg balance under fatigue.

Why It Works: Controlled "overexposures" expand what you can see—and handle.

APPLIED V.I.T.A.L.—VITALITY

Lens Question	Where is my spark fading or shining today?
Metaphor	Vitality is your ISO setting—it adjusts your sensitivity to the light of life. Low ISO dims you. High ISO makes the most of what's available.
Why It Matters	Without vitality, the rest falters.
Data Cue	Most adults lose 3–8% of muscle mass per decade after age 30 unless they actively maintain it. Mobility is use-it-or-lose-it.

Quick Win	Step outside for 5 minutes within 30 minutes of waking—no phone.
Micro-Experiment	Add 1 minute to your usual plank or wall sit; log how you feel.
Practice Cues	Gentle rhythmic movement • Nature immersion • Breathwork

Carmen, sixty-one, began walking at sunrise—not to lose weight but to witness the world wake up. Over time, these walks became a spiritual practice, grounding her and reconnecting her to neighbors and nature.

AUTHOR'S GLIMPSE:

There were mornings I moved just to remember I was still here. A walk with Peaches, a barre class—they weren't just routines. They were lifelines. Vitality, for me, began as survival and grew into something sacred.

Vitality—So What?

Vitality is not about doing more—it's about noticing what brings you to life. You have the right to protect your energy and pursue what restores you. Let your next breath be a choice, not a reaction.

Vitality → Intention. Waking to your body summons energy—but without direction, that energy can scatter. Now we turn to the "why" that turns motion into meaning. Vitality gives you the fuel to move forward; Intention charts where the energy is headed, turning raw strength into purposeful direction.

Vitality dimmed when I ignored the quiet cues.

[I] INTENTION: LIVING IN ALIGNMENT

Once energy is restored, the question becomes where it's meant to go—and this section turns toward the quiet power of choosing how to move, not just where.

Intention depletes in ways both subtle and sharp. Physically, it shows up as scattered routines, unfinished practices, or the restless body that moves without direction. Emotionally, it arrives as indecision, distraction, or the quiet erosion of purpose—when choices feel reactive instead of deliberate. These signals are not failures; they are reminders that intention must be renewed, not assumed.

The shadow of Intention is rigidity or drift. When intention hardens, it becomes inflexible—locked into routines that no longer serve, mistaking stubborn adherence for purpose. When intention fades, it dissolves into distraction—choices made reactively, without coherence or clarity. In both shadows, the compass of purpose is lost, reminding us that true intention is not about control or passivity but about living with deliberate direction.

I've felt both rigidity and drift in my own routines. Some mornings, I sit quietly after my warm-up, letting the stillness settle in before the rush of the day begins. It's in that space—between movement and motion—where intention lives. Not in the "to-do list" but in the why beneath it.

I didn't always think about life this way. Like many, I chased productivity—mistaking activity for alignment. But over time—through reflection, sweat, setbacks, and silence—I began to realize that moving forward means very little if you don't know where you're going or why you're going there.

That's when I started designing my days rather than reacting to them. It began with journaling. What started as a place to track workouts and jot reminders eventually grew into a tool of quiet accountability. I could ask myself hard questions and not flinch. Was I showing up for the things that mattered? Was I living according to my values—or just filling time?

Intention is the bridge between meaning and motion. It's the reason I warm up before I even begin my day. It's the reason I reset my morning routine when it starts feeling stale. Recently, I swapped in wooden ring push-ups and horse stances—not to impress anyone, but because they challenge my stability, both physical and mental. They require presence. And presence is the gateway to purpose.

Intention is also about how I interact—with my family, my body, my past. It's how I've learned to notice when I'm withdrawing because I don't feel heard or when I'm tempted to push too hard just to prove I still can. It helps me pause and ask: What is needed here? Not what's expected, not what's easiest, but what's right.

That question has changed how I approach everything—from money decisions to the way I speak to my adult children. It doesn't mean I always get it right. But it means I'm awake to the fact that there's a choice in every moment. And choice is agency made real.

When I developed V.I.T.A.L. Aging, intention became the spine. Without it, strength has no direction, and longevity risks becoming just survival. But with intention, even the smallest action can become an act of dignity.

So I live with questions, not just answers:

- What is this movement cultivating in me?

- Where am I aiming my energy today?

- Who am I becoming in the process?

And when I'm unsure, I remind myself: I don't need to have it all figured out—I just need to begin the day in alignment with something deeper than momentum.

Intention deepens as we age. It's less about moral perfection and more about wholeness. When our values, actions, and words align, we feel at peace. Without that alignment, aging can bring regret or confusion. With it, aging becomes an opportunity to live more truly.

Intention is the why behind movement. It's the compass, not the engine. Too often we move by default—compelled by habit or obligation. But when intention leads, even small steps become sacred. Living with intention means asking not just what you're doing but why. Why this run? Why this silence? Why this path?

Intention gives direction, but direction alone is fragile. It needs persistence to carry it forward—that is where Tenacity begins.

INTENTION REFLECTION

Intention is the compass beneath your choices. It's the quiet clarity that helps you move with purpose, even when the path is uncertain.

Pause here.

What are you choosing today and why? What values are guiding your decisions, and where might they need recalibration?

Intention doesn't demand certainty—it asks for honesty. Let's begin there.

- What am I currently focusing my "lens" on—and is it aligned with what I value most?

- Where am I scattering energy on subjects that don't belong in the frame?

- If I zoomed in on just one area of my life this month, what would it be?

[•]   **Lens Check for Intention** *(Selective Focus)*

A wide scene is nothing without a focal point. Decide what stays sharp, and let the rest fall away.

Reflection Prompt: Name the one subject in today's frame that truly matters. Let everything else soften.

Micro-Act: Write a single-sentence intention before bed and meet it in the morning light.

APPLIED V.I.T.A.L.—INTENTION

Lens Question	Why am I choosing this movement now?
Metaphor	Intention is your internal navigation system—GPS calibrated by values. When it's misaligned, even the fastest route leads nowhere.
Why It Matters	Intention isn't rigidity. It's the clarity that keeps your choices aligned with what matters.

Data Cue	Research shows that individuals who link physical activity with personal meaning are far more likely to sustain it long-term.
Quick Win	Name one thing you want to feel today—and one action that supports it.
Micro-Experiment	Tonight before bed, write a single-sentence intention on a Post-it and stick it on your bathroom mirror. Read it aloud the next morning before your first task.
Practice Cues	Weekly values journaling • Boundary setting • Relationship inventory

Intention—So What?

Intention is the quiet force behind meaningful action. You don't need to have it all figured out—you just need to know what matters today. Choose one thing. Let it be enough.

Intention → Tenacity. A compass can chart the course, but storms will come. Tenacity is the steady hand that keeps the wheel turning when the sky darkens. Once the destination is set, Tenacity becomes the steady engine that keeps you moving, even when the road is steep or the weather turns.

Intention sharpened when I stared long into the dark.

[T] TENACITY: RESILIENCE THROUGH CHALLENGE

These pages trace the kind of resilience that grows slowly, honestly, and from within—because clarity alone isn't enough; life will always test the frame.

Tenacity depletes in ways that are easy to miss. Physically, it shows up as exhaustion from pushing too hard, injuries born of stubborn repetition, or the body's quiet protest when persistence turns into strain. Emotionally, it arrives as burnout, frustration, or the hollow drive to keep going without clarity—when perseverance slips into noise instead of purpose. These signals are not failures; they are reminders that tenacity must be renewed, not assumed.

The shadow of Tenacity is stubbornness without clarity. When tenacity hardens, it becomes inflexible—pushing past limits without listening, mistaking sheer resistance for resilience. When it frays, it collapses into noise—effort scattered, persistence drained of purpose, motion without meaning. In both shadows, the drive to endure loses its compass, reminding us that true tenacity is not about endless struggle but about purposeful persistence aligned with growth.

Tenacity often gets confused with noise—with grit that shouts or effort that shows. But I've learned that true tenacity is quiet. It's not in the dramatic gestures or viral achievements. It's in the days when you lace up your shoes again, when no one's watching. It's saying: I will keep going, not because it's easy or exciting but because this is who I am.

When I developed the V.I.T.A.L. Aging framework, this principle came into sharp relief. Tenacity is the bridge between intention and outcome. Without it, all the planning in the world dissolves under pressure. With it, even the slowest progress matters.

There were times—especially in the months after my mother's passing—when grief quieted everything. The motivation, the structure, even the desire to show up. But I kept moving. Not always with energy but with resolve. I journaled not to solve anything but to witness it. I did my warm-ups not to improve but to remember that I could still move.

That's tenacity. the refusal to forget who you are.

When I hit a two-minute dead hang this year, it wasn't because I trained with intensity. It was because I trained with consistency. I didn't chase records. I just didn't stop. Tenacity lives in those quiet decisions—to stretch before bed, to step away instead of snapping back, to carry on even when the results seem small or invisible.

It also shows up in relationships. In therapy. In the moments with family when I feel unheard or unseen and still choose to soften instead of harden. Some days, the hardest part isn't the workout—it's the restraint. The willingness to pause and reflect instead of react. That's where emotional tenacity lives. And at this point in my life, it's just as important as anything I do in the gym.

I don't need to be extraordinary. I need to be reliable—to myself, to the people I love, and to the quiet commitments I've made to my future. Tenacity is how I become that person, slowly and surely, day by day.

Tenacity is quiet strength. It's not brute force—it's adaptability. It's learning to show up, especially when progress feels slow. Aging well means learning how to fail well, recover wisely, and keep growing. Tenacity is not about hustle—it's about holding. It's the ability to keep showing up even when your pace slows, your footing shifts, or the wind changes direction.

As we age, discipline changes shape. What used to be brute force becomes breath. What used to be speed becomes consistency. Tenacity is resilience made rhythmic.

Tenacity gives us endurance, but endurance alone is not enough—it needs coherence. That is where Alignment begins.

◉ **Crisis Directive Tool:**

If this chapter stirred memories of your own crisis moments, consider drafting a personal directive. Appendix C offers a customizable template to clarify your needs, boundaries, and support preferences—so you're never left voiceless in a vulnerable moment.

TENACITY REFLECTION

Tenacity is not about pushing harder—it's about holding steady when the winds shift. It's the quiet grit that helps you return, again and again, to what matters.

Before you enter the Lens Questions, reflect:

Where have you shown resilience recently? What helped you persist, and what did you learn in the process?

Tenacity is forged in motion. Let's honor yours.

- What practice do I return to even when motivation fades?

- Where have I "held the shot steady" through challenge, and what did that reveal about me?

- If my life were a long-exposure image, what streaks of light (habits) would appear?

Clarity over time comes from holding steady through noise and motion.

Micro-Experiments:
- Slow a breath cycle to 6–8 per minute during effort.
- Return to one "anchor habit" every day for a week.

Why It Works: Consistency through blur creates the streaks of light that define your long shot.

APPLIED V.I.T.A.L.—TENACITY

Lens Question	What keeps me showing up when it's hard?
Metaphor	Tenacity is your anchor line in stormy water. It doesn't stop the waves, but it keeps your vessel from drifting beyond recovery.
Why It Matters	Tenacity is resilience made rhythmic.
Data Cue	Older adults who maintain consistent movement patterns—even at moderate levels—reduce fall risk and increase lifespan by 22%.

Quick Win	Do the smallest next step of something you've been avoiding—no more than 2 minutes.
Micro-Experiment	Pick one small habit you've let slip (e.g., a 5-minute stretch, a 60-second breathing break). Commit to doing it tomorrow—no performance goal, just consistency.
Practice Cues	Hormetic stressors • Micro-resets • Reframing setbacks

>> Real-Life Barriers to Intentional Aging

Intentional aging doesn't happen in a vacuum. Many people face:

- Chronic illness or physical limitations
- Financial insecurity or housing instability
- Caregiver responsibilities
- Cultural or societal expectations
- Legal or systemic barriers

These challenges don't disqualify you from living V.I.T.A.L.—they make your journey even more vital. The framework is built to flex, offering tools for resilience, clarity, and hope in the face of complexity.

Tenacity—So What?

Tenacity is not about never falling—it's about returning. You've already endured more than you give yourself credit for. Keep showing up. Even gently counts.

Tenacity → Alignment. Persistence alone can feel like pushing a boulder uphill. When grit meets grace—when resolve is guided by awareness—we find alignment. Effort alone isn't enough—Alignment is the compass check, ensuring that your persistence is carrying you toward the right horizon, not just further down the wrong path.

Tenacity surfaced only when the light was gone.

[A] ALIGNMENT: CULTIVATING PRESENCE AND ATTENTION

To pay attention, this is our endless and proper work. —Mary Oliver

Here, I look at how presence becomes a practice—a way of returning to yourself again and again—because strength without steadiness can still collapse, and alignment is what brings the body and mind back into the same frame. Sometimes it begins with noticing a small misalignment in an ordinary choice—reaching for the extra cup of coffee instead of a glass of water, or pushing through fatigue instead of pausing—and correcting it before it compounds.

If intention establishes your values (the *desired* course), Alignment is the daily sensor that checks your integrity (the *actual* current position).

Alignment depletes when body and mind drift apart. Physically, it shows up as imbalance—posture collapsing under fatigue, movement that feels mechanical instead of integrated, or routines that strain rather than support. Emotionally, it arrives as dissonance—values compromised by convenience, choices made without coherence, or the quiet unease of living out of sync with what matters most. These signals are not failures; they are reminders that alignment must be renewed, not assumed.

The shadow of Alignment is dissonance or compromise. When alignment fractures, the body moves one way while values pull another—posture collapses, routines feel hollow, and choices lose coherence. At the other extreme, alignment can harden into false harmony—compromising deeply held principles for convenience, mistaking conformity for integrity. In both shadows, the frame tilts, reminding us that true alignment is not about perfection or appeasement but about living in sync with what sustains both body and spirit.

I've come to believe that strength without alignment is just noise—misapplied energy. But when movement and purpose are aligned—when effort flows from something deeper—that's when real power emerges.

In the gym, alignment is obvious. The difference between a clean squat and a back tweak. Between a steady dead hang and a shoulder strain. It's physical—yes—but also mental. It asks for attention. It punishes force and rewards alignment.

Recently, I've been incorporating horse stances and wooden ring push-ups into my morning practice. These movements demand precision—not the kind that shows up on a stopwatch but the kind you feel in your bones. They require balance, core engagement, and, most of all, humility. You can't muscle your way through a wobbling plank on unstable rings. You have to center yourself. You have to listen.

Alignment is not just posture in the gym or a metaphor for values—it's the daily calibration between what we say, what we do, and what we believe. Misalignment often shows up in subtle ways: the tension in your shoulders when you say "yes" but mean "no," the fatigue after a day spent chasing someone else's priorities, the unease when your calendar doesn't reflect your deepest commitments.

I remember a season when my schedule was full but my spirit was empty. I was moving constantly but not toward anything that mattered. Alignment came back slowly—through small acts of honesty. Saying no to one obligation. Saying yes to a walk with a friend.

Choosing presence over productivity. Each adjustment was like leveling a tripod: small shifts that steadied the whole frame.

That's alignment.

But it's not just in exercise. It's in how I listen to my body when I haven't slept well or how I adjust my schedule when I feel stretched too thin. It's in how I choose conversations that nourish over those that deplete. How I recalibrate after disappointment—not with shame but with care.

I think about my father here—the way he raked the yard with quiet intention, never in a hurry. He didn't just fix things—he tended to them. A loose hinge, a leaning fence, a drawer that stuck—he found a way to keep things going, often with whatever he had on hand. An old hinge became useful again. A spare board found new life. His hands were resourceful but never rushed.

He moved through the world like someone who respected rhythm— of time, of tools, of daily rituals. No wasted motion, no need for applause. Just quiet stewardship. That was his alignment: between effort and purpose, between care and economy.

I carry that memory into my own practice—into wooden ring push-ups that demand patience more than power, into breath-centered movement that insists on listening before acting. Alignment isn't just about posture. It's about presence—moving through the day like it matters, because it does.

That legacy shaped me. Not just how I train but how I live. When I feel out of step—when anxiety spins or frustration simmers—it's often a sign that some part of me is misaligned. That I've made a choice based on fear instead of values. That I've fallen into noise rather than signal.

Alignment calls me back.

In this season of life, alignment also means honoring the interconnectedness of body, mind, and spirit. I train not just to look a certain way but to live a certain way. Strong in posture. Calm in thought. Steady in presence. It's all one system.

That's the heart of this framework. Not optimization, not perfection—just integration. So that the way I move reflects the way I want to be. So that I can carry more than weight—I can carry memory, joy, grief, and hope. Gracefully. Fully. Without fracture.

Alignment is coherence—the felt sense that your outer actions match your inner truths. When aligned, motion becomes flow. Misaligned, it becomes friction. This pillar isn't about perfection. It's about listening: to your joints, your values, and your emotions and making micro-adjustments accordingly.

Alignment steadies us in the present, but the arc of living stretches beyond today. Longevity asks how we sustain meaning across years, not just moments.

> ◉ **Co-Response Checklist:**
>
> *Healing is rarely a solo act. Appendix D provides a practical checklist to help you and your support network cocreate a response plan—one that honors your agency while inviting collaboration. Use it to build trust, clarity, and shared language.*

ALIGNMENT REFLECTION

Alignment is the art of living in sync—with your values, your rhythms, and your relationships. It's not about perfection—it's about coherence.

Pause here.

Where in your life do things feel in harmony? Where do you feel tension or misalignment?

This pillar invites you to recalibrate—not to fix but to flow.

[•] Lens Questions for Alignment (Sync of Actions, Values, Body, and Voice)

- Does the picture I present to others match the one I truly see within?
- Where do my actions blur, creating a double exposure between what I believe and what I do?
- If the emotional tide of my life feels chaotic, where do my actions and values need to come into better sync?

[•] Lens Check for Alignment (Horizon Line)

A level horizon reads as calm and true; tilt feels uneasy.

Micro-Act: Pause three times today for a body-mind scan. Adjust posture, breath, or tone until level returns.

Why It Works: When your inner and outer lines match, the whole frame settles.

APPLIED V.I.T.A.L.—ALIGNMENT

Lens Question	Is my effort in sync with what I value?
Metaphor	Alignment is the horizon line in your creative process. Without stability, even the sharpest lens can't deliver clarity.
Why It Matters	When your breath, body, and belief system move together, you're in alignment.
Data Cue	Emotional dissonance and physical burnout are strongly correlated. Chronic misalignment raises cortisol, blood pressure, and inflammation.
Quick Win	Ask yourself: "Is this mine to carry?" and set down one thing that isn't.
Micro-Experiment	Choose one 5-minute window (e.g., after lunch) for a "body-mind scan": sit quietly, notice tension or hunger or mental noise, then take two full, slow diaphragmatic breaths.
Practice Cues	Stillness rituals • Body + mind scan • Digital sabbaths

AUTHOR'S GLIMPSE:

I used to think alignment meant certainty. Now I know it's about integrity—about choosing what's true even when it's hard. My therapist helped me name the places I'd bent too far. Realignment was painful, but it gave me back my voice.

Alignment—So What?

Alignment is the courage to live in sync with your values. You are allowed to change course when the old map no longer fits. Listen inward. Adjust as needed.

Alignment → Longevity. *Aligned actions are habits, and habits become character. Over time, character shapes the legacy that outlives the moment—that's longevity. When your daily steps are aligned with your chosen course, Longevity becomes possible—the care and pacing that allow you to sustain the journey with dignity over time.*

Alignment found its rhythm when the noise finally ceased.

[L] LONGEVITY: CREATING MEANING AND LEGACY

This section widens the aperture toward the long view, where small acts accumulate into a life with depth—the long arc, the legacy of how we live.

Longevity depletes when the arc of living stretches without renewal. Physically, it shows up as wear that accumulates—joints stiffening, recovery slowing, or the quiet erosion of endurance over time. Emotionally, it arrives as resignation, the sense that days blur together, or the fading of curiosity that once made each season feel alive. These signals are not failures; they are reminders that longevity must be renewed, not assumed.

The shadow of Longevity is survival without meaning. When longevity hardens, it becomes fixation—stretching time for its own sake, mistaking endurance for fulfillment. When it fades, it slips into resignation—days endured rather than lived, curiosity dimmed, and purpose eroded. In both shadows, the arc of living loses its vitality, reminding us that true longevity is not about simply lasting but about sustaining depth, curiosity, and renewal across the years.

Longevity isn't just about adding years. It's about asking: What do those years allow me to become? For some, the goal is to live longer. For me, the goal is to live deeper, longer—to create a life worth sustaining and sharing.

The more I age, the more I understand that legacy isn't something you leave behind. It's something you carry forward. My parents modeled that with quiet consistency. They weren't flashy. They didn't chase status. But they invested—in their work, their family, their values. That planted something in me: a belief that how we live today echoes into someone else's tomorrow.

Longevity also asks us to think about sustainability. How do we pace ourselves so we don't burn out before the finish line? How do we invest in relationships, communities, and practices that will outlast us? It's not about sprinting through life but about walking with enough steadiness that others can walk beside us.

That's why I think of longevity not as survival but as stewardship. I train today not just for myself but for my ability to show up in a decade. To be present at milestones. To carry what matters—whether it's groceries, gear, or a loved one's weight when needed. To help—not just be helped.

There's also a kind of emotional longevity I'm learning. The kind that resists cynicism. That refuses to disengage just because the world feels noisy or uncertain. Every therapy session, every reflective journal entry—it's not just healing the past. It's clearing the ground for something durable to grow.

My fitness practice is a mirror for this. I'm not chasing performance peaks anymore. I'm tending the system. I'm watching how my body adapts to stress, how it recovers, how it adjusts over time. It's less about force, more about finesse. Less about dominance, more about dignity. That's a shift I welcome.

So when I think of V.I.T.A.L. Aging as a whole, this is the horizon it all points toward: a longevity that includes muscle, mindset, relationships, and meaning. A lifestyle that sustains—not just extends.

Because in the end, I want to be remembered not just for what I did but for how I carried myself. And I want to be alive to that memory before anyone else is.

Longevity isn't what we leave behind when we're gone—it's what we live into today. It's how we show up with care and move through the world with presence and purpose. It's the wisdom we share, the impact we grow—in mentoring another, tending a garden, restoring a bond, speaking truth, or practicing daily kindness.

Longevity is not about how long you live—it's about how long your life feels meaningful. It's legacy, yes, but also laughter. It's planning for the marathon, not just the mile. It's making decisions today that your future self will thank you for—the version of you walking into tomorrow more balanced, more forgiving, more free.

Longevity stretches the arc of living, but arcs bend differently across generations. The Hinge Generation asks how comfort and abundance can be carried with resilience, how renewal can be rebuilt rather than inherited. That is where the paradox becomes personal.

LONGEVITY REFLECTION

Longevity is more than survival—it's about building what lasts. It's the quiet layering of choices, rituals, and relationships that shape your legacy.

Before you move into the Lens Questions, take a moment.

What are you carrying forward from this season of life? What would you like to leave behind, and what do you hope to pass on?

Longevity is lived now. Let's explore how.

- What story am I composing for those who will view my photograph after I'm gone?

- Which connections (family, friends, community) bring my picture into sharper focus?

- How can I widen the frame today to include what will still matter 10, 20, 30 years from now?

Widen for connection, narrow for clarity under pressure.

Reflection Prompt: What choice today will still hold value in ten years?

Why It Works: Send one note of thanks or encouragement—plant the seed now.

APPLIED V.I.T.A.L.—LONGEVITY

Lens Question	What impact do I want to leave behind?
Metaphor	Longevity is your aperture over time. It widens to let more light in and narrows to preserve clarity under pressure.
Why It Matters	Longevity honors time without hoarding it. It is grace extended forward.
Data Cue	The strongest predictors of longevity aren't just physical—they include purpose, social connection, and adaptability to change.

Quick Win	Do one small thing your future self will thank you for—60 seconds or less.
Micro-Experiment	Plant something this week—an herb, a flower, or a tree. Notice how tending it changes your sense of time and continuity. Each act of care is a seed for tomorrow.
Practice Cues	Storytelling circles • Mentorship and teaching • Letter writing • Gardening rituals

As we step back and look at the five pillars together, it becomes clear that they are more than concepts to reflect on—they are lenses through which we live, move, and feel. Each V.I.T.A.L. pillar connects not only to a physical practice that strengthens the body but also to an emotional quality that shapes our inner landscape. The table below offers a simple map of these relationships, linking philosophy to movement and emotion so you can see how they work in harmony. Think of it as a quick reference guide—a way to align the lens, body, and spirit before moving forward.

V.I.T.A.L. Pillar	Movement Pillar	Emotional Pillar	Explanation of Link
Vitality	Cardio	Hope/ Energy	Cardiovascular training builds stamina and breath, which fuels vitality. The emotional effect is renewed energy and hope for life's possibilities.
Intention	Balance	Clarity	Balance requires mindful focus. Practicing balance sharpens both physical and mental steadiness, creating clarity of direction.
Tenacity	Strength	Resilience	Strength training demands repeated effort and perseverance. This cultivates resilience—the emotional power to withstand challenges.
Alignment	Mobility	Integrity	Mobility keeps joints, posture, and patterns in harmony. Alignment ensures integrity between inner values and outward action.
Longevity	Flexibility	Legacy	Flexibility preserves adaptability over time. Emotionally, it connects to legacy—leaving behind a story of sustained growth and grace.

This integrated view circles back to the bridge in chapter 2, where core values began their progression into core movement—a reminder that each pillar, domain, and emotional anchor is part of one living framework.

The pillars of V.I.T.A.L. are not a prescription. They're a mirror. A language. A rhythm.

You don't have to master them all at once. Just start tracking your signals. Just listen.

Begin with one question. One stretch. One observation. You don't need a new body—just a new frame.

1. Choose one pillar.
2. Ask the guiding question aloud.
3. Write down what comes up—no judgment.
4. Now move—walk, stretch, breathe—with that answer in mind.

Longevity—So What?

Longevity is built in the small, repeated choices that honor who you are becoming. You are already shaping your legacy—moment by moment. Let today be part of what lasts.

In Simple Terms: The Five V.I.T.A.L. Pillars	
Each pillar is a lens you can pick up when you need it. Some days you'll need more energy, other days more grit, and sometimes just a reminder to realign. Together, they form a framework for living with clarity, purpose, and endurance.	
Vitality	This is your spark. It's the energy that gets you moving in the morning and keeps you going through the day. Vitality is about noticing when your battery is low and recharging before you burn out.
Intention	This is your compass. It's the reason behind your choices—the "why" that makes your actions meaningful. Intention helps you live on purpose instead of drifting through routines.
Tenacity	This is your staying power. It's what helps you keep showing up, even when progress feels slow or the path feels steep. Tenacity is quiet resilience—the strength to keep going when it matters most.
Alignment	This is your balance point. It's when your actions match your values, so life feels steady instead of scattered. Alignment is the sense that what you're doing on the outside fits who you are on the inside.
Longevity	This is your long view. It's the choices that add up over years—the health you preserve, the relationships you nurture, the legacy you leave. Longevity is about building a life that still feels like yours decades from now.

Synergy Table

Below is a compact, easy to scan table showing how each V.I.T.A.L. pillar interacts with the others, what that interaction accomplishes, and one quick practice to strengthen the link before you finish the core text.

Pillar	Interacts With	How the Interaction Helps	Quick Practice
Vitality	Intention; Tenacity	Movement fuels clarity and stamina for sustained effort; prevents burnout	10-minute morning walk; note 1 clear intention
Intention	Alignment; Longevity	Clear purpose guides choices that match values and future goals	Write 1 guiding sentence each morning
Tenacity	Vitality; Alignment	Routine and persistence turn small actions into durable habits	Repeat one small task daily for 7 days
Alignment	Intention; Longevity	Ensures actions reflect values and build meaningful legacy	Pause midday; ask "Does this match my values?"
Longevity	Tenacity; Vitality	Long-term perspective shapes sustainable habits and recovery plans	Do one thing your future self will thank you for

Together, these pillars form a living system—one that adapts as you do.

When the arc of a life aligns with its values, longevity becomes more than years—it becomes meaning carried forward. Yet the story continues. Next we turn to the Hinge Generation, where legacy meets transition and values are tested across time.

That's your V.I.T.A.L. moment. That's how it begins.

CHAPTER 6

THE HINGE GENERATION

{ from muscle to memory }

I remember the first time I carried both a film and a digital camera on the same trip. The film camera was heavy, deliberate; the digital was light, fast, seemingly endless. I didn't know it then, but that moment was a hinge: one foot in scarcity, the other in abundance.

As my own frame widened, I began to see the larger story we're all part of.

This chapter widens the frame to the era that shaped us—the pressures we inherited, the patterns we absorbed, and the possibilities we now carry forward.

Longevity stretches the arc of living, but it is the Hinge Generation that reveals how values bend, adapt, and endure across time. Comfort and abundance, once hard won, can weaken the communal bonds that forged resilience. The habits of prudence, discipline, and sacrifice—born in hardship—often fail to carry forward intact. This is the paradox we inherit: Prosperity gives us ease, but ease erodes the very structures that made prosperity possible.

Here's where the generational story becomes lived experience.

For the Hinge Generation, this paradox is personal. We stand between the scarcity that shaped our parents and the abundance that shapes our children. We've gained the comfort they dreamed of yet often lost the structure that kept them strong. Resilience, for us, cannot be inherited—it must be deliberately rebuilt, not passively received.

I feel this tension daily. My body reminds me of longevity's demands—pace, recovery, patience. Yet my spirit reminds me of the hinge: that comfort without discipline drifts, and discipline without renewal hardens. To live well in this generation is to hold both truths at once.

But there's another way to see this moment.

The hinge is not a burden—it is an aperture. Every generation carries its echoes, but how we respond becomes our frame. What we inherit is not destiny; it is material for recomposition.

These questions sit at the heart of the hinge.

The Hinge Generation asks:
- How do we carry abundance without losing resilience?
- How do we rebuild communal strength in an age of individualism?
- How do we honor legacy while creating new rituals of renewal?

And this is where the personal meets the structural.

This is where V.I.T.A.L. Aging meets history. The pillars are not just personal practices—they are generational tools. They remind us that longevity is not survival but stewardship. And stewardship, in hinge years, means choosing to live with intention, vitality, tenacity, alignment, and renewal—so that what bends does not break.

The metaphor becomes literal here.

That tension in my hands mirrors the tension of a generation. Just as I balanced two cameras, many of us balance two eras—honoring the weight of what came before while adapting to what is emerging. This is the story of the Hinge Generation.

Let's define the hinge more clearly.

Every generation carries its own weight, but some stand at a pivot point—caught between honoring the past and preparing for the future. I call this the Hinge Generation: those who find themselves simultaneously caring for aging parents while still supporting, guiding, or launching children and younger kin. Defined less by a strict age bracket and more by life events and social role, this generation lives at the intersection of responsibility and transition. They are the hinge on which two doors swing—the door closing on one era of family life and the door opening into another.

Here's the hidden cost of living at the hinge.

The Hinge Generation is the primary victim of Deferred Maintenance—the quiet debt of self-neglect that accumulates when serving as the pivot point between generations. The V.I.T.A.L. framework is not just a path to personal fitness; it is the mandatory maintenance schedule for this pivotal moment in your life.

This is where the strain becomes visible.

The greatest pressure point we face is not simply the volume of responsibility but the silent surrender of self-care. In serving as caregivers, providers, and memory-keepers, we often defer their own health, their own dreams, their own renewal. This is where the

V.I.T.A.L. framework offers a lifeline. By emphasizing movement, intentional rest, emotional resilience, and legacy-building, it provides a structure to reclaim agency and dignity in the very season when both feel most at risk.

Let's zoom out for a moment.

This chapter draws a direct line between the generational crisis and the book's core themes. The unpaid bill of vitality is nowhere more visible than in the Hinge Generation, who postpone their own needs in the name of duty. Yet the imperative to reverse the logic of deferral is also most urgent here. To hinge well is not to break under the strain but to integrate strength, flexibility, and care for the self alongside care for others.

And here's the lived reality beneath the data.

The Hinge Generation embodies the paradox of aging with responsibility: They are stretched thin, yet they hold the power to model a new way forward. By refusing to defer their vitality, they can transform what feels like a burden into a legacy of resilience.

A visual helps clarify the tension.

Think of it as a photograph split down the middle: on one side a rusted factory gear, worn smooth by decades of hands; on the other the glow of a circuit board, humming with invisible currents. Gen X is the bridge between those two images—the last to inherit the weight of the gear, the first to navigate the light of the screen. Their story offers a mirror for our own and a reminder of what must be reclaimed as we move forward.

The cameras in my hands taught me that every frame carries both memory and possibility. In the same way, Gen X carries both the weight of the gear and the glow of the circuit board. They are the living hinge between endurance and adaptability.

The story begins with the generations before us.

To understand the weight Gen X carries, we must first look at the forces pressing on the hinge from both sides. On one side stood the Greatest Generation, the Silent Generation, and the early Boomers—shaped by muscle, mobility, and embodied community. Their lives were marked by *Vitality* in motion and *Intention* forged through daily labor, setting the foundation for what came next.

For earlier generations, health and belonging were embodied realities. Daily movement was built into survival—factories, farms, and construction sites kept bodies in constant motion, and in 1970 fewer than 15 percent of Americans lived with obesity (CDC). Community was equally physical: churches, unions, bowling leagues, and neighborhood associations served as "third places" where identity was reinforced and connection was expected. Strength was measured in sweat, and belonging was measured in presence.

The hinge began to move.

But as the hinge began to strain, Gen X came of age. They were the last to inherit the weight of muscle and community and the first to feel the pull of screens, globalization, and shifting social bonds. Their story is one of *Tenacity*—enduring the shock of transition—while searching for *Alignment* between the values they inherited and the new realities they faced.

And the next generation stepped into a different world.

When the hinge finally swung open, Millennials and Gen Z stepped fully into a new reality. The digital tide had risen, reshaping health, belonging, and mobility. What Gen X absorbed as tension, later generations inherited as imbalance—an imbalance that now demands *Intention* in choices and *Longevity* in perspective if it is to be corrected.

But imbalance isn't the whole story.

Yet beyond imbalance lies a subtler danger—one not of scarcity but of surplus. But imbalance is only part of the story. Prosperity itself has become its own paradox.

Sociologically, the prosperity paradox highlights how the prudence, discipline, and sacrifice that define one generation's economic success—habits forged in hardship—often fail to carry forward to the next. In their place, abundance weakens the communal bonds that once held people together, encouraging a natural turn toward self-expression and individualism. For the Hinge Generation, this means resilience cannot be inherited; it must be deliberately rebuilt rather than passively received.

Here's how the paradox shows up in real lives.

The paradox is not only sociological—it is lived. A Gen X reader who finally retires but cannot stop grinding. Someone who has achieved stability yet still feels unsafe. A midlife worker unable to enjoy time off because rest feels like falling behind. Prosperity was supposed to bring ease, but instead it often breeds anxiety, leaving us caught between comfort and unease.

For those of us in the hinge years, the paradox is personal: We've gained the comfort our parents dreamed of yet often lost the structure that kept them strong.

This brings us to the heart of the hinge.

This is why Gen X matters: They are not just another generation in sequence but the hinge itself—the fulcrum where endurance gave way to adaptability, where embodied community gave way to digital connection. They carry the memory of what was lost and the blueprint for what must be reclaimed: *Vitality* in body, *Intention* in purpose, *Tenacity* in change, *Alignment* in values, and *Longevity* in the lives we are building.

Let's name the generation clearly.

GEN X: THE TRANSITIONAL GENERATION

Gen X grew up in both worlds. They were the last children to roam neighborhoods freely and the first adults to navigate the digital revolution. They carried latchkeys in their pockets and later carried pagers, then cell phones.

Their health story reflects the hinge. By 2000, obesity rates had doubled to 30 percent—a number that tells the story of bodies moving less, screens glowing more, and stress rising in ways our parents never imagined. Sedentary lifestyles began to replace physically demanding work. Stress-related illnesses rose as job security waned and globalization reshaped the economy. The body was no longer the primary tool of advancement; the mind, and later the screen, took its place.

Socially, they were the last to inherit robust third places and the first to watch them erode. Robert Putnam's *Bowling Alone* (2000) captured this decline: Civic participation, club memberships, and informal gatherings all fell sharply. Gen Xers remember both the neighborhood block party and the creeping isolation of suburban sprawl. They carry the memory of an embodied community, even as they adapted to its absence.

The hinge didn't stop moving—it accelerated.

AFTER THE INFLECTION:
INFORMATION AND IMBALANCE

With Millennials and Gen Z, the rules changed entirely. The internet democratized access to knowledge, but it also accelerated inequality. Respect was no longer earned through endurance but through visibility, influence, and digital fluency.

The numbers tell their own story.

The costs became clear:

- Health: Today, more than 40 percent of US adults live with obesity—a hinge that has swung from daily movement to daily sitting. Nearly half of young adults report frequent loneliness, a number that paints not just a statistic but a portrait: empty rooms lit by glowing screens, friendships deferred, vitality leaking away.

- Social Belonging: The US surgeon general warned in 2023 that loneliness increases the risk of premature death by 26 percent—as if each day of disconnection were another cigarette smoked. By 2024, the WHO declared social disconnection a global public health threat. These are not abstract warnings; they are the echo of voices gone missing from dinner tables, pews, and playgrounds.

- Third Places: Cafés, libraries, and community centers still stand, but the rituals of gathering have thinned. Where once people lingered, stories now scatter across fragmented feeds. The hinge has shifted from embodied presence to digital drift, leaving us with spaces that exist but no longer anchor.

- Mobility: Millennials are less likely than Boomers or Gen X to out-earn their parents. The ladder of upward mobility has not disappeared, but its rungs are farther apart, its climb more precarious. The hinge here is economic: Where persistence once promised progress, effort now too often meets imbalance.

When the hinge finally swung open, Millennials and Gen Z stepped fully into a new reality. The digital tide had risen, reshaping health, belonging, and mobility. What Gen X absorbed as tension, later generations inherited as imbalance—an imbalance that now demands Intention in choices and Longevity in perspective if it is to be corrected.

Here's the deeper hinge beneath the hinge.

Earlier generations hinged on scarcity, where survival demanded sacrifice. Today's hinge swings on prosperity, where the challenge is not survival but significance. The danger is not lack of resources but lack of reasons. Yet abundance invites us to redefine motivation itself.

For Millennials and Gen Z, the hinge moment is this: to transform prosperity from a source of passivity into a platform for purpose. If scarcity once forged resilience, then prosperity must now forge responsibility. The hinge swings between comfort and contribution, between consumption and creation. To live it well requires not only adaptation but intention—choosing to turn abundance into agency and ease into legacy.

Gen X carries the memory of scarcity. Millennials and Gen Z inherit the challenge of abundance—learning how to live meaningfully when everything is already within reach.

If Gen X was the hinge between the rusted gear and the glowing circuit board, then Millennials and Gen Z live in the glow of the touchscreen—bright, responsive, and endlessly abundant, yet fragile the moment the power fades. The touchscreen offers infinite choice with a single tap, but it also tempts us to mistake access for achievement and scrolling for significance. It is the perfect symbol of modern prosperity: dazzling in its immediacy but demanding intention if it is to become more than distraction.

This is the hinge's legacy.

WHY GEN X MATTERS

Gen X absorbed the shock of transition, and the hinge still bears their imprint. They straddle two measures of worth: respect once earned through sweat and relevance now tallied in digital fluency. In their bodies, the strain shows as a slow leak of vitality—stress rising, movement fading, health deferred. In their neighborhoods, it appears as the fraying of connection—the block party remembered, the cul-de-sac gone quiet, the third place digitized.

And yet, Gen X carries something rare: the memory of belonging. They remember when presence was participation, when stories were told face to face, when community was lived, not curated. That memory is not nostalgia—it is a blueprint. It reminds us that the hinge need not break under strain. It can swing forward with Vitality, Intention, Tenacity, Alignment, and Longevity.

Gen X's story is not just history—it is a mirror. Their leak of vitality and fraying of connection are the same pressures many of us feel in our own bodies, calendars, and communities. The hinge is not only generational, it is personal. The questions Gen X raises are also yours. What we inherit is not just the shape of their struggles but the light they learned to hold.

Every generation writes its own code, but most of us inherit the bugs. We debug our parents' errors while introducing our own, patching systems built for different operating conditions. The work is less about rewriting everything than learning how to run old logic in a new environment—without crashing what still works.

Now bring this into your own frame.

REFLECTION BRIDGE: A GENERATIONAL LENS

That first trip with both a film and a digital camera taught me something I didn't realize at the time. Holding two tools—one heavy and deliberate, the other light and endless—wasn't just about photography. It was a glimpse of what it feels like to live at a hinge: one hand on the weight of the past, the other on the speed of what's coming.

Generations carry that same duality. Gen X, in particular, has lived it in their bodies, their work, and their communities. They remember the sweat of embodied community—block parties, union halls, church basements—and they've adapted to the glow of screens, remote work, and digital connection. They are the hinge between endurance and adaptability.

But the hinge is not only generational. It's personal. Each of us feels the strain of carrying two worlds at once: the discipline of scarcity and the distraction of abundance. The question is how we steady ourselves in that tension.

- Health: Where do you feel the hinge in your body—strength or fatigue?
- Connection: Which third places once grounded you? How might you reclaim belonging now?
- Work and Legacy: How can you honor hard work without letting it drain you?
- Prosperity: Do you live more by scarcity's resilience or abundance's distraction?
- Scarcity teaches resilience; abundance demands intention. Which shapes your hinge today?

The hinge does not close on us; it opens before us. The question is whether we will drift through abundance or step through it with intention, carrying forward the dignity of effort into a new age of meaning.

This is the aperture the chapter leaves you with.

Like carrying both cameras, we are always holding two ways of seeing: the careful frame chosen with intention and the endless stream available in an instant. To live this hinge well is to steady our hands, choose what is worth capturing, and let the blur itself become part of the story.

That is the story of Gen X—not a clean break but a hinge in motion. A reminder that our second act is not about choosing one image over the other but about holding both: the endurance of muscle and the adaptability of memory. To live this hinge well requires a new kind of maintenance, one that the V.I.T.A.L. framework makes possible.

The prosperity paradox proves that we can no longer rely on external pressure to forge character. The V.I.T.A.L. framework is the deliberate act of replacing the accidental rigor of scarcity with the intentional discipline of meaning.

- Vitality keeps the body moving, restoring energy where it leaks away.
- Intention directs our choices, ensuring we live by design rather than default.
- Tenacity sustains us through change, not as stubborn resistance but as resilient adaptability.
- Alignment brings our actions into harmony with our deepest values so that effort and meaning move in the same direction.
- Longevity reminds us that the choices we make today ripple forward, sustaining not only our years but the quality and dignity within them.

The hinge does not have to creak under strain. With Vitality, Intention, Tenacity, Alignment, and Longevity, it can swing with purpose—carrying us forward into a second act defined not by deferral but by strength, dignity, and hope.

Every generation carries its echoes, but how we respond becomes our aperture. What we inherit is not destiny—it is material for recomposition.

ONE-PAGE V.I.T.A.L. SNAPSHOT

Pillar	Core Meaning	Metaphor	Guiding Question	Quick Win
[V] Vitality	Energy for life through movement, recovery, and rhythm	ISO settings—sensitivity to life's light	Where is my spark fading or shining today?	Step outside for 5 minutes within 30 minutes of waking—no phone
[I] Intention	Purpose and direction in every action	Internal GPS—calibrated by values	Why am I choosing this movement now?	Name one thing you want to feel today—and one action that supports it
[T] Tenacity	Quiet, consistent resilience	Anchor line—holds steady in storm	Is my effort in sync with what I value?	Do the smallest next step of something you've been avoiding—no more than 2 minutes
[A] Alignment	Coherence between values and actions	Emotional tide—flows strong and clean when aligned	Is my effort in sync with what I value?	Ask yourself: "Is this mine to carry?" and set down one thing that isn't
[L] Longevity	Creating lasting meaning and legacy	Aperture over time—widening/narrowing for clarity	What impact do I want to leave behind?	Do one small thing your future self will thank you for—60 seconds or less

Grief to Generativity

I crossed the finish line, and the race shifted into repair. The blackout closed the shutter on my life; confinement taught me how to develop the image in the dark. In a cell no larger than a closet, survival stopped being abstract and became practice—small, deliberate acts that steadied a frayed system. The pillars of V.I.T.A.L. were not theory then but tools: the routines, breaths, and margins that rebuilt a life frame by frame.

What follows isn't a timeline but a convergence—moments returning out of order as they often do once the lights come back on.

AFTER THE BLACKOUT

Some moments arrive quietly but open a larger frame.

A flyer arrived in the mail yesterday addressed to Mom: *The Loneliness Epidemic.* I should have recycled it. Instead I opened it slowly, read it deliberately, and let it sit in my hands. The paper breathed new energy into Project V.I.T.A.L.; the idea began to take shape on the page—layout, form, structure—moving from thought into vessel. As the words settled, I asked myself: What last image do I want to leave the reader with?

That question pulled me back to where the shift began.

September 30 reads in my journal like a transition photograph—no longer employed, not yet retired; not drowning but treading. I wasn't panicked. I was present. Deliberate. I kept showing up—for myself, for Mom, for the legacy my parents entrusted me with.

And then the frame narrowed again.

In November my mother died. After her funeral, in a parking lot, I pressed the shutter and everything went dark: the seizure closed the frame on the life I thought I knew. The blackout set a chain in motion. In the months that followed, the collapse rippled outward into a crisis that stripped away my freedom. In July I was incarcerated; that chapter remains unresolved and is still moving through the courts. I name it plainly because it is part of the arc: collapse, confinement, and the slow, stubborn work of repair.

But even in the darkroom, small lights appeared.

What followed was a messy, tender apprenticeship in small practices: yoga with Ayden, a grounding barre class, a thoughtful text from Taylor. Loss kept arriving—Uncle Lou, Pat, a neighbor, a friend—and still I kept moving. I curated collages of Mom and Dad's life not to tidy grief but to order it: make time legible, make meaning visible. A digital assistant could sort a thousand photos by face and sharpness; only I could see which frames mattered.

Slowly, the image began to reveal itself.

Then, like an eye adjusting to sudden light, I began to develop the image. The blackout and the confinement taught the same lesson: when the world narrows, the smallest acts become the architecture of survival. A morning stretch. A sentence in the margin. A counted breath. These were not niceties; they were practical tools.

With time, the practices became a way of seeing.

A new year arrived, and I signed up for a Stoic challenge. Day two asked for a word. I offered *present*. The AI suggested *resilient*. Both fit. In that moment I saw myself clearly—not failing, not floating, but becoming. The job offer that followed came when I was ready, not desperate. Alignment felt like a shutter speed slowing: clarity, intention, exposure.

But healing is never linear.

Now the calendar reads July again, but the month carries a different weight. July is the month I was incarcerated; it is also the month I learned how to keep a life going in the smallest of spaces. Some parts of that story remain unsettled. I say that because honesty matters: Not all endings are neat, and not all verdicts are final.

And still, the story keeps unfolding.

I am not finished becoming. I have barre tomorrow and therapy after that. I have splits to reclaim, pistols to balance, a handstand to chase. I have stories to write, data to map, and a legacy to live into.

This is where the framework finds its roots.

Project V.I.T.A.L. is not a tidy theory. It is a postscript written in margins and margins again—a set of practices that held me when everything else was stripped away. It is the framework I inherited from my parents, from loss, from love, and from the hard work of staying present while the outcome is still unknown.

And now the frame widens to include you.

If anything in these pages helps you steady a day, borrow it. If it doesn't, leave it in the margin and try something else. The work of repair is ongoing, and some questions remain unsettled. I name that so the book closes with honesty.

In the end, the work returns to the smallest tasks.

So I keep framing—one small, deliberate act at a time. If you ever lack a pen, remember there is always a margin to write in.

What I Carry Forward

This is not an addition to the story but what remained once it settled into practice.

> **READER'S CHALLENGE**
>
> You've explored the V.I.T.A.L. pillars in thought. Now, live them. Begin your own spiral with the *One-Week V.I.T.A.L. Experiment*. Each day invites movement, reflection, and legacy-building. Whether you walk, write, stretch, or rest—do it with intention. The spiral is yours to shape. Let it carry you forward.

Before we go further, the frame darkens.

Note: This postscript includes references to mental-health crisis and incarceration.

Here's where the story returns to its origin.

Challenges don't stay on the page; they arrive in life's unpredictable turns. The blackout was the moment my body gave way—consciousness slipping into darkness. Months later that collapse had become a crisis that stripped away my freedom. Incarceration turned survival into practice: rhythm, agency, and the smallest acts of presence—one stretch, one sentence, one counted breath—kept me steady. From that necessity the V.I.T.A.L. pillars emerged as a survival map, not theory but practice.

Only later did I understand what those months were teaching me.

Looking back, the blackout and the months that followed taught me what truly matters: small, consistent acts of care, the courage to name needs, and systems that meet people where they are. The pillars of V.I.T.A.L. are not abstract ideals—they are the practices that held me. Carry them forward in whatever form fits your life.

But honesty required widening the frame again.

I accept my part in that day. What I also accept is that systems can fail people in crisis. There could have been other paths: on-scene medical response, co-responder teams pairing clinicians with law enforcement, and community de-escalation resources—practical alternatives worth piloting and scaling.

And then reality inside these walls was stark.

Incarceration left me with almost no choices. Isolation was stark—minimal contact, puréed meals, and, in my last two weeks, only two brief turns at recreation. Anger hummed in the air, dulled but never gone. I couldn't change the system, only how I stood inside it.

Still, even there, a small aperture opened.

When I finally borrowed a pen, I wrote in the margins of the Rules & Regulations. Turning a book meant to define my limits into a place for my own words felt like quiet defiance.

This is the moment the pillars took shape.

That's when V.I.T.A.L. stopped being theory and became a survival map. In a space no larger than a closet, each pillar revealed itself in practice:

- Vitality: Move each day, however small, so the body remembers it is alive.
- Intention: Choose one deliberate action that anchors the day.
- Tenacity: Keep a routine when motivation fades.
- Alignment: Pause to ensure actions reflect values.

- Longevity: Act with tomorrow in mind, building habits your future self can trust.

And those practices became more than survival.

Those small acts were my form of defiance—against despair, against stagnation, against being defined by my worst day. They steadied me and kept me moving toward dignity, hope, and possibility.

What emerged from that season is a different kind of commitment.

I leave this book committed to recovery, advocacy, and practical change. My story is one thread in a larger fabric of how we respond to mental-health crises. If sharing it sparks honest conversation—among law enforcement, clinicians, families, and communities—then some good can grow from what was, for me, the hardest season of my life. We can build responses rooted in safety, compassion, and dignity. That is the work in front of me now, and it's work I will carry forward—pen in hand, page by page.

And still, the work returns to the smallest acts.

The spiral continues—one small, deliberate act at a time. If you ever lack a pen, remember: There is always a margin to write in.

Now the frame turns toward legacy.

WHAT I CARRY FORWARD

Those margins taught me a final lesson.

And in those margins, I discovered something more: What matters most is not only what I've carried but what I choose to carry forward. That choice—the daily act of deciding what endures—is the true work of V.I.T.A.L.

I carry forward the quiet lessons that don't always make it into data tables or training logs:

- the way a morning walk steadies my breath
- the way a handwritten note restores connection
- the way a pause can be as powerful as a push

And I carry forward the people who stretched me.

I carry forward the memory of those who shaped me—parents, mentors, friends—whose presence still guides my choices. Their voices remind me that strength is measured not only in muscle but in patience, kindness, and the willingness to begin again.

The pillars remain my companion.

I carry forward the five pillars of V.I.T.A.L. not as abstractions but as companions:

- Vitality as the spark that keeps me moving.
- Intention as the compass that keeps me true.
- Tenacity as the rhythm that keeps me steady.
- Alignment as the horizon that keeps me level.
- Longevity as the long view that keeps me hopeful.

And beneath it all is a deeper belief.

I carry forward the belief that even in loss or disruption, we are never finished. Each day is a frame to compose, a choice to make, a story to tell.

This is the part I offer outward.

I carry forward the invitation—to myself and to you—to live with agency, to honor what restores, and to leave behind not just years but meaning.

And this is the aperture the postscript leaves open.

In the end, what we carry forward is not only our story but the light we pass on.

Now the practice becomes yours.

NEXT STEPS: LIVING V.I.T.A.L.

You've read the pillars. You've seen them in practice. Now it's your turn to spiral them into your own life. Start small, stay steady, and let each step build on the last.

1. Choose One Pillar Each Day

Vitality → Move your body in a way that feels alive; try a 10-minute walk or gentle stretch.

Intention → Begin the day with one deliberate choice; name it aloud or write it down.

Tenacity → Keep a routine, even when motivation dips; repeat one small task at the same time each day.

Alignment → Pause once today to check if your actions match your values; ask one quick question: "Is this true to me?"

Longevity → Do one thing your future self will thank you for; make one small, future-focused decision.

2. Capture It in the Margins

Write a single line each day—on a sticky note, in a journal, or even in the "margins" of your calendar. Let it be your proof of practice.

3. Share the Light

Tell someone what you're carrying forward. A text, a call, a note—legacy grows when it's spoken aloud.

Remember: The spiral is yours to shape. One small act is a frame in the larger story you compose.

Roots and Branches

What follows is not a conclusion but a pause—an invitation to step forward in your own time.

Before I close, I return to where the story opened.

Some objects stay with us long after the moment passes.

I step into this epilogue still holding that borrowed pen—not the plastic barrel itself but what it gave me: proof that words could still be mine. The margins that once hid my survival notes are now wide-open pages, and with each line I write, I claim more space in my own story.

And so, I turn to the two people who shaped the frame.

Dear Mom and Dad,

This letter has been waiting in me for years.

I've thought about writing this letter for a long time. Maybe I've been writing pieces of it my whole life—through journal entries, through photographs, through the quiet choices I've made in your honor.

I want you to know: I've been paying attention.
To the way you lived.
To the sacrifices you made without fanfare.
To the way you showed up—day after day, year after year.

You taught me more through action than words. You gave me a life where I had the time and freedom to reflect, to grow, to chase meaning beyond mere survival. You gave me a foundation strong enough to fall apart and rebuild upon.

But love is often dearest in its absence.

This past year has tested me in ways I wasn't ready for. Saying good-bye to both of you has been like living in a negative space—seeing the shape of love by what's missing. But in the stillness, I also found clarity. I realized that your story didn't end when your frames went black. It continues—in the way I move, the way I care, the way I build.

From that loss, something steady began to form.

Project V.I.T.A.L. was born from that realization. It's my way of making sense of what you gave me:

Vitality—in every breath and every movement.
Intention—in how I show up and why I keep going.
Tenacity—in every quiet act of endurance.
Alignment—in living a life that reflects what I value.
Longevity—in honoring time, not just counting it.

Your lessons didn't end—they took root.

I move through the world now carrying your lessons in my bones.
I see your faces in strangers' kindness, in my own quiet strength,
in the soft echo of your voices when I get still enough to hear them.
I no longer rush to avoid grief. I walk with it—and find grace.

And the metaphor becomes literal again.

You gave me the lens. I'm still framing the world with it.

With all my love,
John

What followed was its own kind of grace.

Healing rarely happens alone.

As I settled into this new rhythm of carrying grief instead of outrunning it, I started noticing the people who were quietly shaping my healing. It surprised me at first—how the right person can enter your life at the exact moment a lesson is ready to land. My parents had always taught me through presence, through consistency, through the way they moved in the world. After they were gone, others began to teach me too, often without realizing it.

The lessons came quietly at first.

Their arrivals were subtle—small, almost forgettable moments that reveal their meaning only in hindsight. Yet each of these women carried a quality my parents once modeled so effortlessly. Through them, V.I.T.A.L. stopped being something I practiced in isolation and became something relational, reciprocal, alive.

And then three unexpected teachers appeared.

In that season of rebuilding, three remarkable women—all whose names begin with "J"—stepped into my story, each one illuminating a different pillar of V.I.T.A.L., each one reminding me that the framework wasn't just something I designed on paper. It was something lived. Something shared.

The first illuminated intention.

The first was a stranger—a young data-science hopeful I mentored as she found her footing in a new field. Her curiosity, her openness, and her hunger to learn sparked my Intention pillar—the why behind each step I take. Though our paths drifted apart, I still imagine us sitting side by side one day, notebooks open, reconnecting the early bridge we began to build.

The second rekindled vitality.

Next came my barre instructor and trainer—an embodiment of Vitality. Her energy pushed and refined my own five movement pillars: strength in every lift, cardio in every beat, flexibility through each stretch, mobility with each transition, and balance in every wobble. In helping me rebuild my body, she helped me reclaim agency, and I hope V.I.T.A.L. will one day return that gift to her in her own teaching.

The third brought alignment and tenacity back into focus.

Finally, my therapist steadied my Alignment and whispered Tenacity when I wavered. She witnessed V.I.T.A.L. unfolding session by session—my moods rising and falling like shutter speeds—yet each opening of clarity reveals deeper coherence. Through her guidance, she created a feedback loop of trust and growth, helping me integrate what I had long carried alone.

Together, they reminded me of something essential.

I thank them not only by name but by the pillars they helped reignite. Each encounter reminded me that we heal in community and that the lessons our parents began can continue in unexpected forms. Their presence showed me that V.I.T.A.L. was never meant to be practiced alone; it's a shared rhythm of movement, intention, resilience, alignment, and purpose.

And beneath their lessons was a deeper truth.

I've come to believe that every encounter, whether fleeting or enduring, joyful or fraught, carries the potential for grace. Not perfection, not resolution, but grace: the quiet dignity of showing up, the courage to listen, the humility to part without harm. This book is one such encounter. As we approach its final pages, I return to that intention: May our meeting begin and end with grace—a quiet, complex kindness that doesn't demand resolution. If you've found resonance here, let it be a soft landing. If you've found a challenge, let it be a kind one.

Now the frame widens to include you.

The next step begins here—in whatever margin you choose to fill. With movement. With meaning. With grace.

And so the stage circles back to light.

Light spills across the frame, catching in the smallest details until the whole picture breathes. I've carried that frame for as long as I can remember— not just in photographs but in the way I see the world. It was a gift from my parents before I knew to name it, a way of noticing that turned moments into meaning. I didn't know then how often the light would change or how many times I would have to learn to hold the frame steady in the shadows.

CODA

Here is the final aperture.

As I've shared my story, I hope you've started to see how these principles can also shape yours. And so the frame holds steady—what began as my parents' gift has passed through my hands into others', and will, I hope, keep passing on. Their quiet steadiness still guides the way I hold the lens. The lens is still here, still clear, still catching the *light—spilling across the frame*, illuminating the smallest details until the whole picture breathes.

Just like the way morning light once slipped through a narrow window.

Fade to black. Begin again.

And there is the truth I return to.

The light never left.
I only had to learn how to move again.

Take a breath before you turn the page.
Let what you've noticed settle.

Fade to black. Begin again.

ONE-WEEK V.I.T.A.L. EXPERIMENT

Living the Spiral with Intention, Movement, and Meaning

- Each day invites you to engage with one or more V.I.T.A.L. pillars: Vitality, Intention, Tenacity, Alignment, Longevity.
- Every prompt includes:
  - Movement—physical or emotional
  - Reflection—a journal cue or question
  - Legacy Action—a small step toward lasting impact

Day	Movement	Reflection	Legacy Action
1: VITALITY—Honoring What Energizes You	Take a walk in silence. Let your thoughts settle.	What activities or relationships make you feel most alive?	Reach out to someone who energizes you and express gratitude.
2: INTENTION—Choosing the Path	Do a 20-minute intentional activity (stretching, cooking, organizing) with no multitasking.	What are you choosing today and why?	Set one intention for the week and share it with someone you trust.
3: TENACITY—Embracing the Process	Complete a workout, walk, or task that challenges you.	Where have you shown grit recently? What helped you persist?	Document a moment of perseverance—write it, voice it, or share it.
4: ALIGNMENT—Living in Sync	Block off one hour for something that nourishes you.	Where are your actions aligned—or misaligned—with your values?	Say "no" to one thing today that doesn't serve your deeper goals.
5: LONGEVITY—Building What Lasts	Revisit a place that holds meaning (physically or in memory).	What do you want to be remembered for this season?	Create a small artifact—photo, recipe, note, or object—that reflects your current legacy.

Day	Movement	Reflection	Legacy Action
6: INTEGRATION—Connecting the Spiral	Do something that blends two V.I.T.A.L. pillars (e.g., train with intention, reflect with agency).	How do your pillars interact? Where do they reinforce each other?	Share one insight from your week with someone else—start a conversation.
7: RESTORATION—Honoring the Cycle	Rest intentionally—nap, read, soak, or simply breathe.	What did this week teach you about your rhythm?	Write a closing journal entry or letter to yourself titled "What I'm Carrying Forward."

Practice Companions

This appendix is designed as a companion to the reflections in chapter 3. While the chapter invites you to consider renewal as a way of living, the following activities provide tangible steps to embody those ideas. Here you'll find curated lists of practices and a thirty-day challenge, each crafted to help you move from insight to action. Think of this section as a resource: a place to experiment, adapt, and discover what renewal looks like in your daily rhythm. Use it flexibly—return to it when you need inspiration, or follow it step by step as a structured journey toward agency and vitality.

The following matrix offers a spectrum of activities, each engaging different domains of movement. Use it as a map—notice where your strengths lie and where renewal might invite you to explore new territory.

Activity	Strength	Cardio	Flexibility	Mobility	Balance
Alpine Skiing	7	7	6	8	7
Animal Flow	8	6	8	9	8
Barre	7	4	8	7	9
Baseball	6	5	5	6	7

Activity	Strength	Cardio	Flexibility	Mobility	Balance
Basketball	7	8	6	8	8
BodyBalance	6	5	9	8	8
BodyPump	8	6	2	4	6
Bouldering	9	5	6	8	9
Calisthenics	8	6	7	7	7
Cheerleading	8	7	8	7	8
Classic Barre	5	2	9	6	8
Cross-Country Skiing	6	10	5	7	6
Cycling	3	8	2	3	4
Dancing	6	7	7	8	7
Fencing	7	7	6	8	9

Activity	Strength	Cardio	Flexibility	Mobility	Balance
Football (American)	8	7	5	6	6
General Strength Training	9	6	3	4	6
Gymnastics (All-Around)	7	7	10	9	9
HIIT	8	10	4	6	6
Hiking	6	6	4	5	7
Ice Skating	6	7	5	8	10
Judo (Sport/ Competition)	8	6	6	8	7
Karate (Mixed Kumite + Kata)	7	7	6	7	7
Marching Band	6	7	3	6	7
Parkour	6	8	7	10	8
Pickleball	5	6	4	7	8

Activity	Strength	Cardio	Flexibility	Mobility	Balance
Pilates	6	4	8	7	7
Powerlifting	10	1	1	2	3
Racketball	8	8	4	7	8
Rock Climbing (Sport/Lead)	8	6	7	8	9
Rollerblading	5	8	4	9	9
Rowing	7	7	4	5	4
Running (5K)	4	9	3	4	5
Running	4	9	3	4	5
Sitting Meditation	1	1	2	1	2
Slacklining	2	2	5	6	10
Snowboarding	7	8	6	7	8

Activity	Strength	Cardio	Flexibility	Mobility	Balance
Snowshoeing	6	7	4	6	6
Soccer	7	9	6	8	7
Softball	5	4	6	5	7
Stationary Cycling	3	8	2	1	4
Swimming (Lap Pool)	6	8	5	6	1
Swimming (Front Crawl)	7	10	6	7	6
Synchronized Swimming	7	8	8	7	7
Taekwondo (WT Sparring + Poomsae)	6	8	8	7	7
Tai Chi (General Form)	5	3	8	9	9

Activity	Strength	Cardio	Flexibility	Mobility	Balance
TRX Suspension Training	8	6	4	7	8
Tennis	6	7	5	8	8
Volleyball	6	7	5	8	7
Wrestling	9	8	7	8	8
Yoga	5	3	9	8	7
Zumba	6	9	6	8	7

THIRTY-DAY CHALLENGE ACTIVITIES MATRIX

These thirty-day challenges provide structured pathways. They are not prescriptions but invitations to experiment with rhythm, discipline, and discovery.

Below is a comprehensive list of popular thirty-day fitness challenges, each rated on a 1–10 subjective scale across the five movement domains (1=minimal engagement; 10=maximal engagement).

Challenge	Strength	Cardio	Flexibility	Mobility	Balance
30-Day Push-Up	7	3	2	3	4
30-Day Sit-Up	6	2	2	3	3
30-Day Squat	7	3	4	5	6
30-Day Plank	8	1	1	2	3
30-Day Dead Hang	5	1	1	2	5
30-Day Wall Sit	4	1	1	1	2
30-Day Burpee	8	10	3	6	5
30-Day Jump Rope	5	10	3	5	4
30-Day Mile-a-Day	4	9	3	4	5
30-Day Running	4	9	3	4	5
30-Day Ab (Crunch)	5	2	2	3	3

Challenge	Strength	Cardio	Flexibility	Mobility	Balance
30-Day Glute (Butt)	7	4	4	5	6
30-Day Pull-Up	9	2	2	3	5
30-Day Lunge	6	3	4	6	7
30-Day Yoga Flow	5	3	9	8	7
30-Day Walking	3	5	4	5	6
30-Day HIIT	8	10	4	6	6

HOW TO USE

- Rate each domain immediately after your daily challenge session.
- Track your scores over thirty days to visualize where you're consistently strong or under-challenged.
- Identify gaps (e.g., low flexibility), then layer in complementary activities (yoga, Pilates, mobility drills).
- Aim to bring every domain at least into the moderate range (4–6) each week for balanced development.

Remember: Renewal is not about perfection across all domains but about balance, curiosity, and growth. Let these tools serve as companions on your journey.

Movement Domain Reflection

The following movement domains translate the V.I.T.A.L. pillars into physical and emotional practice. While the pillars describe the philosophy of vitality, the domains describe how that vitality moves through the body. They're not identical, but they're related—each domain expresses one aspect of the framework in motion. Together, they offer a way to notice, measure, and recalibrate how you're living the principles day to day.

Instructions: Rate each domain from 1 to 5 based on current engagement (1 = rarely, 5 = consistently). Use the notes section to reflect on what's working and what needs adjustment.

Domain	Description	Score (1–5)	Notes/Observations
Vitality	Physical energy, strength, and stamina. Includes cardio, strength training, etc.		How does movement affect your energy level?
Intentionality	Purposeful movement tied to goals or rituals. Includes barre, yoga, walking.		Are your routines aligned with personal meaning?
Tactile Regulation	Sensory grounding through touch, breath, or proprioception.		Do you use movement to calm or center yourself?

Domain	Description	Score (1–5)	Notes/Observations
Affect Expression	Movement as emotional release or storytelling. Includes dance, journaling walks.		Does movement help you express or process emotion?
Linkage	Movement that fosters connection—group classes, walks with others, caregiving.		Are you moving with others or in community?

Monthly Reflection Prompt

Which domain feels strongest right now? Which one needs attention? What small shift could help rebalance your movement ecosystem?

Crisis Directive Template

CRISIS DIRECTIVE TEMPLATE

Purpose: to help individuals and families prepare for a mental-health crisis with clarity, dignity, and alignment.

This directive organizes information and intentions through the V.I.T.A.L. framework—cultivating Vitality, Intention, Tenacity, Alignment, and Longevity even in moments of distress.

Example:

You feel your breath shortening during a difficult conversation. Your shoulders rise, your jaw tightens. Instead of reacting, you pause.

- Vitality: one slow exhale
- Intention: "what outcome do I want here?"
- Tenacity: stay steady for three more breaths
- Alignment: check in with your values
- Longevity: ask what choice you'll still be proud of tomorrow

One cycle.

Five steps.

A different ending.

VITALITY—Signals and Early Warning Signs

→ *Recognize shifts in energy and balance*

Checklist	Examples/Guidance
☐ Identify 3–5 early signs that indicate a crisis may be emerging.	E.g., disrupted sleep, rapid speech, withdrawal, pacing, missed meds.
☐ Describe what "low energy" or "high agitation" looks like for you.	Helps responders distinguish baseline from crisis.
☐ List sensory sensitivities (noise, light, crowds).	Allows environment to be adjusted early.

INTENTION—Preferred First Responders

→ *Clarify who leads with trust and calm.*

Field	Details
Name:	
Role (therapist, peer, family, etc.):	
Phone/Email	
Preferred Order of Contact:	1. 2. 3.
Preferred Communication Style:	(Text/Call/In-person)
Tip: Clearly stating who should respond first reduces confusion and ensures a compassionate entry point.	

TENACITY—Stabilizing Actions

→ *List grounding practices that restore rhythm and control.*

Domain	What Helps
Movement	Walk, stretch, breathwork, rocking, dancing.
Environment	Quiet room, dim lights, favorite blanket, music, weighted vest.
Medication	Name dosage, location, timing.
Food/Hydration	Snack preferences, water access, avoid caffeine or sugar if triggering.
Sensory Tools	Fidget object, cold water, essential oils, grounding texture.
Note: "Regulation before resolution." Calm body → clear choices.	

ALIGNMENT—Medical and Legal Notes

→ *Ensure clarity between care preferences and medical safety.*

Information	Details
Diagnoses:	
Medications:	
Allergies/Contraindications:	
Advance Directive or Crisis Plan on File (Y/N):	
Consent to Share Info with Responders (Y/N):	

Health-Care Proxy/Legal Guardian:	
Preferred Hospital or Crisis Center:	
Tip: Keep a copy of this section with your ID or care binder for quick reference.	

LONGEVITY—Post-Crisis Plan

→ *Transform recovery into renewal.*

Checklist	Examples/Guidance
☐ Notify therapist or primary clinician within 24 hours.	Reinforces continuity of care.
☐ Schedule follow-up appointment within 7 days	Prevents relapse and supports integration.
☐ Debrief with family / support team.	Discuss what helped and what needs revision.
☐ Update directive as needed.	Keeps plan current and responsive.
☐ Celebrate progress, however small.	Honors resilience; closes the loop on crisis.

QUICK REMINDERS

- **Vitality:** Notice the first signs of imbalance.
- **Intention:** Lead with trusted voices.
- **Tenacity:** Ground through movement and breath.
- **Alignment:** Communicate clearly and safely.
- **Longevity:** Reflect, learn, and recalibrate.

This V.I.T.A.L. Crisis Directive supports dignity, self-awareness, and continuity across care systems. Keep one copy with the individual, one with family or therapist, and one accessible to first responders.

Co-Response Checklist

CO-RESPONSE CHECKLIST FOR LAW ENFORCEMENT AND CRISIS TEAMS

Goal: to reduce escalation and increase safety during mental-health emergencies by emphasizing calm communication, collaborative options, and continuity of care.

Before Arrival

Checklist	Guidance/Rationale
☐ Confirm if medical or peer support is available to co-respond.	Clarify team roles before arrival to avoid overlap or confusion.
☐ Review known history (if available).	Note triggers, medications, preferred contacts, or previous crisis plans.
☐ Ask caller: "What has helped in the past?"	Gather relational data, not just clinical facts; record for on-scene briefing.
☐ Identify a single lead communicator.	Minimizes conflicting messages and maintains a calm tone.

On Scene

Checklist	Guidance/Rationale
☐ Assess for immediate safety (weapons, self-harm risk).	Maintain exit routes and clear space; avoid crowding or cornering.
☐ Use calm, nonthreatening posture and tone.	Maintain eye level, open stance, steady breathing; avoid rapid movements.

☐ Ask individual: *"What do you need right now to feel safe?"*	Centers autonomy and reestablishes trust.
☐ Offer movement options (walk, sit, stretch).	Gentle movement can release tension and restore emotional regulation.
☐ Avoid unnecessary restraint unless safety demands it.	Explain each step if restraint is required; release as soon as feasible.
☐ Consider medical sedation only if de-escalation fails.	Requires medical oversight; document justification and monitor effects.
☐ Use the individual's name and pronouns.	Reinforces dignity and recognition of personhood.
☐ If peers or family are present, designate one calm spokesperson.	Prevents multiple voices from escalating confusion or stress.

Alternatives To Arrest

Checklist	Guidance/Rationale
☐ Mobile crisis team referral.	Provides specialized support in the least restrictive setting.
☐ Voluntary transport to crisis-stabilization center.	Promotes cooperation and preserves agency.
☐ On-scene medical evaluation.	Ensures health issues are ruled out before legal action.
☐ Family-led de-escalation with support.	Strengthens community bonds and reduces trauma.
☐ Notify mental-health liaison for follow-up within 24 hours.	Supports continuity of care and accountability.

Aftercare

Checklist	Guidance/Rationale
☐ Provide written summary of incident to family or caregivers.	Include triggers identified and responses that were effective.
☐ Offer referral to mental health or peer-support services.	Confirm acceptance or preferred provider; ensure handoff.
☐ Document what worked for future response planning	Share securely with local crisis coordination network if available.
☐ Schedule inter-agency debrief within 72 hours.	Allows review of response quality and responder well-being.
☐ Identify lessons for continuous improvement.	Supports V.I.T.A.L. principles of alignment, learning, and longevity.

TONE AND TECHNIQUE QUICK REMINDERS

- Pause before posture. Lead with listening.
- Name emotion, not behavior.
- Safety is shared; calm is contagious.

This checklist reflects trauma-informed, person-centered principles consistent with the V.I.T.A.L. framework: Vitality, Intention, Tenacity, Alignment, and Longevity.

A Deeper Look At the V.I.T.A.L. Framework

You don't have to master everything in these pages. Think of this appendix as a reference library—something to return to when a pillar feels dim, when a shadow state lingers, or when you need a new way forward.

Take what you need. Let the rest wait until you're ready.

Why a deep dive?

The five pillars of V.I.T.A.L. are intentionally crafted to be both practical and easy to remember. Yet beneath their simplicity lies a dynamic system—like the interlocking gears of a camera, each pillar subtly influences the others, each contributing to the full picture of healthspan and resilience.

Appendix E serves as your V.I.T.A.L. field kit: a reliable touchpoint for recalibration, inspiration, or a fresh perspective on your practice. Whether you've just recognized a "shadow state" that needs rebalancing or you're refining a pillar that's already strong, this quick-reference guide gathers the essentials in one place. Use it in real time, during reflection, or as part of a weekly check-in to keep your mind-body-lens system attuned, adaptive, and aligned.

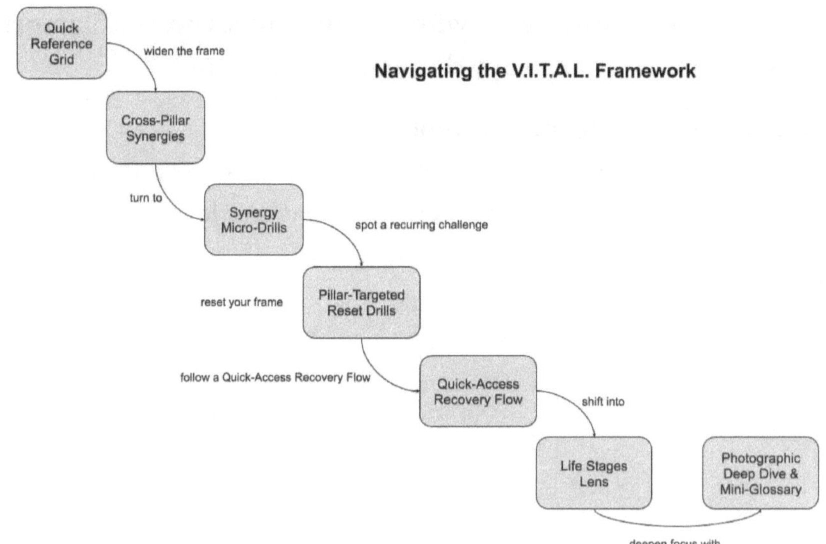

WORKED EXAMPLE WALK-THROUGH

Scenario: Jordan, a mid-career designer, notices a persistent afternoon slump: mind feels "foggy," body sluggish. This matches a shadow state under the Intention pillar—loss of clarity and creative drive.

Step 1—Identify

- Pillar: Intention
- Movement Deficit: lack of balance practice
- Emotional Shadow: distraction, mental drift

Step 2—Select

- From the Synergy Micro-Drills Table: Intention + Alignment — "Lens Shift"
- Movement blend: brisk lateral step-throughs + single-arm reaches toward a high target

Step 3—Apply

- Daily 2 p.m. reminder; perform at a moderate pace focusing on smooth balance transitions and purposeful gaze

Step 4—Observe

- By Friday, sharper focus within 5–10 minutes post-drill; more sustained creative energy through late afternoon

Step 5—Re-evaluate and Anchor

- Mark "Lens Shift" as a go-to reset; anchor it to the photographic cue "Selective Focus" (focus ring + aperture) for quick recall

V.I.T.A.L. Worked Example—Quick-Fill Card

→ *Open Aperture: widening the frame for brighter detail.*

Step & Prompt	Your Notes
Scenario Briefly describe the situation or challenge.	
1—Identify Pillar: Movement Deficit: Shadow State:	
2—Select Drill name(s): Reason for choice:	
3—Apply When/where/how; timing, pace, cues	
4—Observe Changes in body, mind, mood	
5—Re-evaluate & Anchor Keep, adjust, or replace? Metaphor/visual cue:	
Optional Prompt What surprised you most?	

QUICK REFERENCE GRID—PILLARS AT A GLANCE

Pillar	Core Emotion	Movement Domain	Primary Metaphor (Photographic)	Shadow State
Vitality	Energized confidence	Strength + endurance	Sunlit trail cutting through a dense forest	Burnout/ depletion
Intention	Focused clarity	Precision + alignment	Archer in sharp focus mid-draw, blurred background	Distraction/ drift
Tenacity	Determined resolve	Resistance + persistence	Mountain climber gripping an icy ledge at sunrise	Stubbornness/ rigidity
Alignment	Harmonious integration	Posture + coordinated flow	Compass resting on an open map, both perfectly centered	Fragmentation/ misalignment
Longevity	Grounded patience	Sustained capacity + rhythm	Lighthouse beaming through fog toward a distant shore	Complacency/ neglect

Five pillars with core emotion, movement domain, photographic metaphor, and shadow state—your at-a-glance foundation.
- Once you've oriented to each pillar here, widen the frame to *Synergy Micro-Drills* to see how they combine in motion and mindset.

Resilience isn't built in isolation—it's forged in the interplay between domains. The Synergy Micro-Drills table offers quick, targeted practices that blend two V.I.T.A.L. pillars at a time, activating movement and emotion in tandem. Each drill is designed for 3–5 minutes of intentional reset, using metaphor as a bridge between body and meaning. Whether you're navigating stress, seeking clarity, or simply re-centering, these drills offer portable, potent tools for realignment.

SYNERGY MICRO-DRILLS

Pillar Pair (Synergy Name)	Movement Blend	Emotional Target	Quick Drill (3–5 min)	Photographic Connector	Framework Connector
Vitality + Intention (Embodied Purpose)	Dynamic mobility + gaze anchoring	Energized focus	Step-through lunges with head turns toward a fixed point	Wide-angle sweep—openingperspective	Compass & horizon
Vitality + Alignment (Grounded Flow)	Mobility circuit + posture reset	Grounded readiness	Side-to-side reach with spine lengthening and core engagement	Tripod lock—stable, balanced base	Bridge span
Vitality + Tenacity (Resilient Drive)	Power move + sustained hold	Steady drive	20-sec fast-feet burst, then 10-sec balanced hold, repeat	Time-lapse sequence—endurance over time	Tidal rhythm
Vitality + Longevity (Sustained Spark)	Uplift move + expansive gesture	Inspired sustainability	Squat to tall reach with arms opening outward	Panorama sweep—capturing the long view	Passing the torch
Intention + Alignment (Purposeful Balance)	Balance flow + reach to focal point	Clear, aligned focus	Lens shift: brisk lateral step-throughs with single-arm reaches toward a high target	Focus ring + aperture – selective focus	Focus ring + aperture (selective focus)
Intention + Tenacity (Focused Grit)	Controlled exertion + mindful release	Composed persistence	Slow push-up to forearm plank, exhale and relax shoulders	Shutter press-and-hold—steady capture" under next column.	Drawbridge open/close

Pillar Pair (Synergy Name)	Movement Blend	Emotional Target	Quick Drill (3–5 min)	Photographic Connector	Framework Connector
Intention + Longevity (Enduring Intention)	Vision-setting stance + forward step	Commitment to endurance	Stand tall, set gaze ahead, step forward with deliberate posture	Horizon framing—composing the long shot	Planting the flag
Alignment + Tenacity (Steadfast Center)	Spine elongation + loaded carry	Upright stability	Overhead reach with light weight, then walk 10–15 steps	Vertical frame—holding tall lines	Lighthouse stance
Alignment + Longevity (Harmonized Horizon)	Posture alignment + shared gesture	Mutual trust	Stand in partner mirror pose, open arms outward	Depth of field—keeping all layers in focus	Open gates
Tenacity + Longevity (Durable Resolve)	Repeated effort + symbolic close	Enduring contribution	Three rounds of controlled lifts, finishing with hands over heart	Continuous mode—sustained series	Sealing the pledge

Ten pillar pairings with quick reset sequences and dual metaphor connectors to integrate action and imagery.

Spot a recurring challenge? Cross-check with the Shadow States to choose a corrective drill that resets your frame.

The pillars of V.I.T.A.L. rarely act alone. They lean on each other, sometimes in harmony, sometimes in tension. When two pillars intersect, they create a synergy—a dynamic space where energy, values, persistence, presence, and legacy either reinforce one another or reveal imbalance.

To help you notice these intersections, I've expanded the Synergy Table. Think of it as a calibration map: Each pairing comes with a guiding question, a micro-drill, and signals to watch for. Use it when you feel scattered, fatigued, or simply curious about where your energy is flowing.

This is not a scorecard. It's a mirror. Choose the questions that resonate most, notice the emotional signals, and experiment with the micro-drills. The recovery phrases are short mantras you can carry into your day—anchors to remind you that hope, agency, and dignity are always within reach.

V.I.T.A.L. SYNERGY TABLE

Synergy Pair	Reflection Question	Micro-Drill	Emotional Signal	Recovery Phrase
Vitality + Intention	Do I feel energized by the direction I'm heading, or am I moving without purpose?	10-min walk + 1-line compass journal	Restless, scattered	Energy with purpose
Vitality + Tenacity	Am I sustaining my energy through challenge or burning out before I finish?	Movement + hydration + rest check	Fatigue, dread	Endure with rhythm
Vitality + Alignment	Does my physical rhythm match my values, or am I pushing through misalignment?	Breathwork + values scan	Tension, shallow breath	Move in sync
Vitality + Longevity	Am I investing my energy in things that will matter long-term or just reacting to the moment?	Legacy action + recovery ritual	Busy but unfulfilled	Spark with meaning

Synergy Pair	Reflection Question	Micro-Drill	Emotional Signal	Recovery Phrase
Intention + Tenacity	Do I persist in what matters most, or am I stuck in routines that no longer serve me?	Break down goal + recommit	Stuck, disengaged	Purposeful persistence
Intention + Alignment	Are my choices clearly rooted in my values, or am I drifting from what I believe in?	Reflect + adjust one habit	Unclear, conflicted	Values in motion
Intention + Longevity	Is my current path building the legacy I want, or am I postponing meaningful impact?	Write a note to future self	Aimless, disconnected	Legacy with direction
Tenacity + Alignment	Am I showing up consistently in ways that reflect who I am or just grinding through?	Repeat a routine + reflect on its value	Mechanical, joyless	Resilience with integrity
Tenacity + Longevity	Is my persistence shaping something lasting, or am I enduring without direction?	Revisit long-term goal + micro-step	Worn down, uncertain	Endure with vision
Alignment + Longevity	Do my daily actions reflect the legacy I hope to leave, or is there a disconnect between presence and purpose?	Pause + gratitude + legacy action	Drifting, misaligned	Meaningful presence

The Synergy Table is not meant to be filled out once and forgotten. It is a living companion, a way to notice where your pillars are leaning and how they can be recalibrated. Some days you may find yourself energized but unfocused, other days persistent but misaligned. Each pairing offers a question, a drill, and a phrase to steady you. Return to this table weekly, monthly, or whenever life feels unsettled. Let it remind you that balance is not perfection—it is presence. By naming your signals, practicing your drills, and carrying forward your recovery phrases, you reclaim agency in the moment and dignity in the process. Hope grows when you choose to engage, and each small act becomes part of your larger design for healthspan.

The next page offers a simple way to put this into practice. It translates the Synergy Table into a one-page reflection you can use whenever you need clarity. Think of it as a quick check-in: a way to name your signal, identify the synergy pair beneath it, and choose the micro-drill that brings you back to center.

EMOTIONAL SIGNAL: SYNERGY PAIR REFLECTION PAGE

Instructions:

Use this page to identify your current emotional state and map it to the appropriate V.I.T.A.L. synergy pair. Follow the guided questions and record your reflections below.

1. Current Emotional Signal

What are you feeling right now? (Check one)

- ○ Low energy (fatigue, heaviness, numbness)
- ○ High energy (restlessness, agitation, urgency)

2. Narrow It Down

If low energy, select one:
- ○ Overwhelm / lack of direction → Vitality ↔ Intention
- ○ Discouragement / loss of momentum → Vitality ↔ Tenacity
- ○ Feeling disconnected / misaligned → Vitality ↔ Alignment
- ○ Feeling stuck / time slipping → Vitality ↔ Longevity

If high energy, select one:
- ○ Scattered urgency / impulsiveness → Intention ↔ Alignment
- ○ Overexerting / rigid effort → Intention ↔ Tenacity
- ○ Future worry / anxious planning → Intention ↔ Longevity
- ○ Frustration with slow progress → Tenacity ↔ Longevity
- ○ Pushing past limits → Tenacity ↔ Vitality
- ○ Pulled in many directions → Alignment ↔ Longevity

3. Identified Synergy Pair

Write your synergy pair here: _______________________

____

____

4. Micro-Drill Selection

List 1–2 micro-drills you will use to regulate or restore this synergy:

1.____

____

____

2.____

____

____

EMBODIED SYNERGIES IN PRACTICE

The following brief vignettes illustrate how the pillars interact in everyday life. Each story captures a moment when two domains align—and what happens when that balance begins to shift.

Vitality ↔ Intention—Shutter Speed and Aperture

Energy ↔ Focus

Pamela had been waking up tired for months, scrolling before sunrise, drinking coffee that never seemed to land. One morning she left her phone on the table and stepped outside barefoot. The air was cool, the sky still gray. She took one photograph—nothing special, a fencepost catching early light—and felt her breath settle.

It wasn't the picture that mattered but the act of framing it. In slowing down to notice, her energy found a direction. Vitality wasn't something to summon; it was waiting behind attention.

Starting the next morning, she began each day the same way—one mindful frame before opening her inbox. A small aperture for the day to begin.

Reflect:
- Where does your energy scatter when your focus drifts?
- What small, mindful act could open your own day's aperture?

Stability ↔ Flow

Michael prided himself on routine. The same five a.m. run. The same breakfast. The same drive. But lately, his knees ached, and the morning loop felt more like a burden than a rhythm. One day he stopped at the park bench halfway through and simply sat—watching the pond ripple with wind.

In that pause, something subtle shifted. Discipline wasn't failing him; it was asking to evolve. Tenacity without alignment had become rigidity. When he returned to running a week later, he changed his route—same distance, different path. The steadiness remained, but it could breathe again.

Now, before each run, he checks in with his body first—listening, leveling, then locking in.

Reflect:
- Where in your life has steadiness become stiffness?
- What would it look like to keep your rhythm but change your route?

Balance ↔ Perspective

Gina was sorting through old prints for an exhibit—landscapes she'd shot decades ago. Her first instinct was to critique every imperfection: blown highlights, uneven horizons, too much grain. But then she noticed something else—the consistency of her gaze. She had always chased the same light.

Time hadn't blurred her vision; it had deepened it. Alignment wasn't about staying identical—it was about staying true. As she arranged the prints, she saw her life's work as one continuous exposure, slowly widening its frame. The long view revealed not decline but coherence—the art of seeing differently over time.

She decided to print one photo from each decade, not as a timeline but as a single composition—her legacy in motion.

Reflect:
- What patterns or passions have remained constant across your seasons of life?
- How might widening your frame change how you measure progress?

Intention ↔ Longevity—Patience That Reveals

Focus ↔ Endurance

Brian's garden had gone wild during his mother's illness—vines overtaking the fence, soil cracked from neglect. After the funeral, he spent days pulling weeds, too numb to know what else to do. A week in, he noticed small green shoots returning where he'd cleared the ground.

He hadn't realized that tending was its own kind of prayer. The garden wasn't a project to finish; it was a long exposure of care. Intention gave shape to the work, but patience revealed the life beneath it.

He began each morning watering one section, not to restore the garden overnight but to remember that presence itself was growth

Reflect:
- Where in your life could steady attention replace urgency?
- What are you cultivating now that might take years to bloom?

Each synergy lives as a rhythm—action and awareness, effort and ease. When one pillar dominates or fades, the loop begins to distort. What follows are the shadow states that emerge when balance is lost and how to find your way back to center.

WHEN PILLARS ARE MISSING (SHADOW STATES)

Missing Pillar	Movement Deficit	Emotional Shadow
Vitality	Weak cardio capacity	Fatigue, despair
Intention	Lack of balance practice	Confusion, distraction
Tenacity	Limited strength	Fragility, giving up
Alignment	Restricted mobility	Inner conflict, instability
Longevity	Poor flexibility	Short-term thinking, regret

Common expressions of each pillar's imbalance—cues to watch for in thought, posture, and momentum.
- When you've identified a shadow pattern, shift to *Pillar-Targeted Reset Drills* to rebalance your stance and mindset.

PILLAR-TARGETED RESET DRILLS

Pillar	Trigger Cue	Anchor Movement	Breath Pattern	Mental Reframe	Completion Check
Vitality	Heavy, sluggish start; low posture	Stand tall, feet hip width, sweeping arm arcs overhead to open chest	Inhale 3, exhale 3 through nose	"Energy is circulating; I am awake in my body."	Posture upright, breath steady, eyes bright
Intention	Scattered focus; skipping steps	Plant feet, clasp hands at heart center, slow half turns left/right	Inhale 4, hold 2, exhale 4	"I move with clarity and intention."	Calm alignment, reduced fidgeting
Tenacity	Giving up mid-task; shallow breathing	Forward lunge pulses, engaging thighs and core	Inhale 2, exhale 4 forcefully	"I hold steady under pressure."	Muscles active, gaze set, jaw unclenched
Alignment	Crooked stance; imbalance between upper/lower body	Wall-assisted heel-to-crown lengthening stretch	Inhale 5, exhale 5	"Every part of me supports the whole."	Even weight on feet; shoulders/hips squared

Pillar	Trigger Cue	Anchor Movement	Breath Pattern	Mental Reframe	Completion Check
Longevity	Rushed pace; neglecting sustainable effort	Gentle rolling walk in place, controlled heel-to-toe	Inhale 4, exhale 6	"I move for today and tomorrow."	Rhythm feels unforced; tension in calves/low back eased

Corrective sequences designed to restore each pillar's optimal state in both mind and body.
- Complete the cycle by returning to the *Quick Reference Grid* and noting how your pillar's presence feels post-reset.

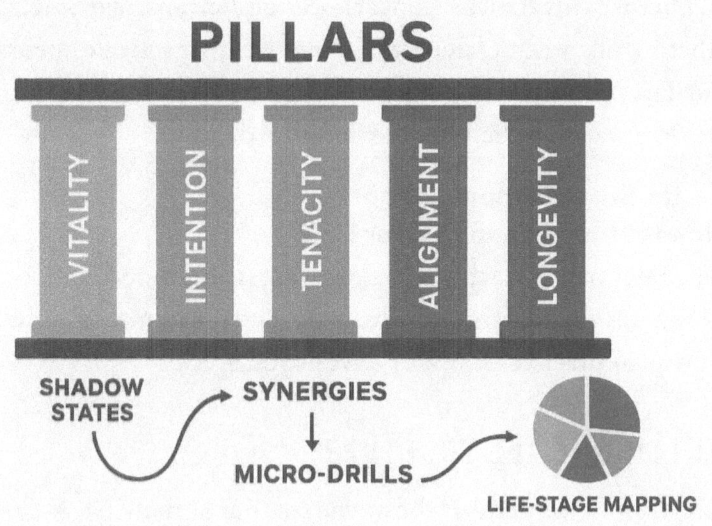

SIDEBAR: HOW TO READ THE V.I.T.A.L. PILLAR INTERACTION GRAPHIC

This diagram shows how the five V.I.T.A.L. pillars work together as a living system. Each component supports the next, creating a loop of awareness, action, and adaptation.

1. Pillars (Top)—Your Core Capacities

Vitality, Intention, Tenacity, Alignment, and Longevity form the structural foundation of this framework. They represent the strengths that support healthy aging and purposeful living. No pillar stands alone—each affects the others.

2. Shadow States (Left)—Early Warning Signals

When a pillar is depleted, it expresses a predictable "shadow" pattern—exhaustion, drift, rigidity, fragmentation, or stagnation. These shadow states help you notice when something needs attention.

3. Synergies (Center)—Where Pillars Work Together

Pillars strengthen one another. Vitality fuels Intention. Tenacity stabilizes Alignment. Longevity widens perspective. Synergy is where resilience grows and where balance is restored.

4. Micro-Drills (Lower Center)—Small Actions, Big Shifts
Micro-drills are brief, repeatable practices that activate or restore a pillar. They translate insight into movement—helping you recover from shadow states and reinforce synergistic patterns.

**5. Life-Stage Mapping (Right)—
How Priorities Change Over Time**
The relevance of each pillar shifts across adulthood. Life-stage mapping helps you understand which capacities matter most right now and how your practices should evolve as you age.

PUTTING IT ALL TOGETHER

The flow of the graphic shows the rhythm of the V.I.T.A.L. system:

Pillars → Shadow States → Synergies → Micro-Drills → Life Stages → back to Pillars.

It's a reminder that growth is cyclical, not linear—and that movement, awareness, and intention work best when they work together.

Quick-Access Recovery Flow

Step	Trigger Cue	Action	Target Outcome
1. Pause & Notice	Sudden tension, imbalance, loss of focus	Stop movement; take 1–2 slow breaths	Shift from reactive to responsive state
2. Ground & Align	Feeling unstable or scattered	Adjust stance/ posture; engage core	Physical stability and mental centering
3. Reset Pillar	Specific muscle fatigue or overcompensation	Apply Pillar-Targeted Reset Drill for affected area	Restore pillar function and symmetry
4. Integrate Breath	Shallow or erratic breathing	Inhale through nose, exhale fully	Oxygenation and nervous system regulation

Step	Trigger Cue	Action	Target Outcome
5. Re-engage Task	Ready to resume movement or focus	Return to activity with refined form	Improved performance and reduced strain

Step-by-step sequence for regaining balance quickly after disruption, blending movement and mindset.
- Complete the cycle by returning to the *Quick Reference Grid* and noting how your pillar's presence feels post-reset.

The V.I.T.A.L. framework adapts across time. Whether you're building, rebuilding, or mentoring, this lens shows how each pillar shifts in emphasis as your life evolves.

LIFE STAGES LENS

Life Stage	Dominant Pillar	Movement Expression	Emotional Growth
Youth	Vitality	Cardio	Hope, energy
Early Adulthood	Intention	Balance	Clarity, choice
Midlife	Tenacity	Strength	Resilience, perseverance
Later Adulthood	Alignment	Mobility	Integrity, wisdom
Elderhood	Longevity	Flexibility	Legacy, grace

- For seasonal or phase-based practice themes, explore *Triple Synergy and Seasonal Blends*—your wide-angle for the year.

The following explores how three V.I.T.A.L. pillars can intersect to support different life seasons—physical, emotional, and environmental.

TRIPLE SYNERGY AND SEASONAL PILLAR BLENDS

Season / Life Phase	Pillar Trio	Movement Blend	Emotional Target	Metaphor Connector
Spring Emergence & Renewal	Vitality + Alignment + Intention	Rhythmic cardio + dynamic mobility + goal-oriented drills	Energized clarity	Panorama Sweep—wide, flowing capture of new terrain
Summer Expansion & Expression	Tenacity + Vitality + Longevity	Load-bearing strength + expressive movement + sustained breathwork	Bold contribution	High-Key Exposure—bright, unapologetic presence in the frame
Autumn Harvest & Refinement	Intention + Alignment + Longevity	Precision holds + balance work + reflective walking	Focused gratitude	Leading Lines—guiding attention toward what matters most
Winter Consolidation & Resilience	Stability + Tenacity + Alignment	Breath-anchored endurance + slow transitions + adaptive flow	Grounded adaptability	Long Exposure—patient capture that reveals hidden depth

- Anchor your seasonal focus with the photographic cues in the *Photography Deep Dive* and *Mini-Glossary* for lasting recall.

How to Use This Table

- Seasonal Practice Planning: Choose the trio that matches your current life phase or external season, and build your weekly movement around it.
- Emotional Calibration: Use the emotional target as a journaling prompt or check-in theme.
- Metaphor Anchoring: Let the metaphor guide your mindset—whether you're zooming out, locking in, or softening into stillness.

PHOTOGRAPHY DEEP DIVE—FRAMING THE JOURNEY

Just as a skilled photographer chooses lenses, exposure, and composition to tell a story, we can use these techniques to shape our own aging journey. Each photographic concept here links directly to the five V.I.T.A.L. pillars—Vitality, Intention, Tenacity, Alignment, Longevity—turning abstract ideas into vivid, actionable images. These metaphors are more than wordplay: They sharpen our focus, broaden our view, and help us capture resilience in every frame of life.

V.I.T.A.L. Pillar	Camera Element	Meaning
Vitality	ISO	Adaptive sensitivity; sets the rhythm and pace of response to conditions
Intention	Focus peaking, histogram	Guides precise targeting and self-regulated exposure to input
Tenacity	Central crosshairs, AF point indicators	Locks onto the goal; maintains unwavering direction
Alignment	Electronic level indicators, grid overlays	Holds spatial and emotional equilibrium; keeps true lines
Longevity	Aperture	Chooses what remains in focus over time; defines lasting story

PHOTOGRAPHY MINI-GLOSSARY— SEEING THROUGH A WIDER LENS

Photography isn't just about cameras—it's a language of light, framing, and focus. In the V.I.T.A.L. framework, we borrow these terms as metaphors you can feel in your body and mind. Just as a photographer adjusts aperture, shutter speed, or focus to capture the clearest image, you can adjust your routines and perspective to bring life into sharper view.

This glossary is your quick-reference guide:

- Plain-language definitions that remove the intimidation of jargon
- Everyday parallels so you can see how each term lives outside of the camera
- V.I.T.A.L. links showing how the concept maps to intentional aging, movement science, and mindset resets

Use it like a lens cloth—a small tool that keeps your view clear whether you're looking through a viewfinder or at the arc of your own day.

PHOTOGRAPHY MINI-GLOSSARY

Term	Visual Cue	V.I.T.A.L. Pillar Link	Metaphoric Tie-In
High-Key Exposure	Bright, evenly lit image with minimal shadows	Vitality + Tenacity	Bold, unapologetic action; flooding life with energy and resilient light
Panorama Sweep	Ultra-wide scene capturing varied terrain	Vitality + Alignment	Embracing shifting horizons while staying grounded in flow
Tripod Lock	Camera fixed on three legs, unmoved by conditions	Tenacity + Alignment	Anchored strength that holds steady through challenge
Zoom Ring Glide	Smooth, precise focal change on the lens	Alignment + Longevity	Shifting perspective without losing clarity over time
Long Exposure	Light trails or softened motion over time	Intention + Longevity	Patience that reveals hidden detail and enduring purpose
Leading Lines	Natural or architectural lines guiding the eye	Intention	Directing focus toward what matters most; eliminating visual clutter
Depth of Field	Foreground sharp, background softly blurred	Intention	Knowing where to focus while allowing nonessentials to fade

Term	Visual Cue	V.I.T.A.L. Pillar Link	Metaphoric Tie-In
Backlighting	Subject illuminated from behind, creating glow	Longevity	Emerging with presence despite uncertainty
Visual anchors and photography-inspired cues to deepen pillar embodiment and recall. • Use these visual anchors while reviewing the *Cross-Pillar Synergies* to deepen both imagery and action.			

These tables are not just for reference—they're for reflection, recalibration, and realignment. Choose one drill this week. Try it. Feel it. Then write your own. The framework lives through you.

AUTHOR'S GLIMPSE

This book began as a way to make sense of what went dark, but it ends as an invitation—to see differently, to move with awareness, to honor the light that keeps returning. What I've learned is that vitality isn't something we hold on to; it's something we participate in. Each breath, each small act of attention, is a kind of aperture, widening us to life as it is.

If these pages have offered you a rhythm, a moment of stillness, or a reason to move again, then we've already met in motion. And that is where the real story continues—in the quiet, deliberate choices you make long after the book is closed, in the way you carry your own light forward.

V.I.T.A.L. in Practice

This section offers snapshots of how the pillars show up in real contexts—not as a checklist but as a lens to return to. These examples aren't exhaustive or hierarchical; they're simply moments where V.I.T.A.L. moves beyond the page and into daily life. Use what resonates, skip what doesn't, and let these scenes help you orient yourself in your own season.

The framework began as a way to rebuild my life after a hinge moment, but its usefulness extends far beyond movement or recovery. Vitality, Intention, Tenacity, Alignment, and Longevity are ways of orienting yourself in the world—helping you move through uncertainty, make deliberate choices, and live with agency and dignity.

V.I.T.A.L. works much like a good design pattern: Once you understand the structure, you can reuse it across different parts of your life. Just as a developer refactors messy code into something cleaner and more functional, V.I.T.A.L. helps you refactor habits, assumptions, and routines that no longer serve you. It's pattern recognition for the human experience—a way to see what's repeating, what's breaking, and what needs to be rewritten with more intention.

This appendix offers examples of how the framework can be applied across different domains. Think of them as reusable components—ideas you can adapt, extend, or modify as your life evolves. Use what resonates. Leave what doesn't. Return whenever you need to debug, redesign, or realign.

1. Physical Well-Being and Movement

Vitality – Reclaim energy through small, consistent movement

Intention – Choose activities that support your body's needs

Tenacity – Build resilience through repetition and recovery

Alignment – Move with awareness, not autopilot

Longevity – Create sustainable routines that support aging with dignity

Movement becomes a way of orienting yourself, not just exercising.

2. Emotional Regulation and Mental Well-Being

Vitality – Notice emotional energy and fatigue

Intention – Name what you feel and what you need

Tenacity – Stay with discomfort long enough to learn from it

Alignment – Respond rather than react

Longevity – Build practices that support long-term steadiness

This is where motion and emotion meet. Small acts create internal space.

3. Personal Finance and Financial Literacy

Vitality – Understand your financial baseline

Intention – Spend and earn in alignment with values

Tenacity – Build habits that compound over time

Alignment – Stay honest with your numbers

Longevity – Plan for future stability and dignity

Money becomes a tool for agency, not anxiety.

4. Career, Work, and Purpose

Vitality – Identify what energizes or drains you

Intention – Make choices that reflect your values

Tenacity – Navigate setbacks with resilience

Alignment – Ensure your work matches who you are becoming

Longevity – Build a career that supports your life, not the other way around

V.I.T.A.L. helps you move through transitions with clarity.

5. Relationships and Communication

Vitality – Notice the energy you bring into relationships

Intention – Communicate with purpose, not impulse

Tenacity – Repair ruptures with patience

Alignment – Show up as your truest self

Longevity – Build relationships that endure through honesty and care

Connection becomes a practice, not an accident.

....

6. Creativity and Personal Projects

Vitality – Protect your creative energy

Intention – Choose projects that matter to you

Tenacity – Keep going when momentum dips

Alignment – Create from authenticity, not comparison

Longevity – Build a sustainable creative life

Creativity becomes a form of movement—a widening of the frame.

....

7. Habit Formation and Lifestyle Design

Vitality – Start with what gives you energy

Intention – Build habits that reflect your values

Tenacity – Embrace repetition and imperfection

Alignment – Adjust habits as your life shifts

Longevity – Create routines that support long-term well-being

Habits become anchors, not obligations.

8. Aging and Life Transitions

Vitality – Maintain strength and presence

Intention – Choose how you want to age

Tenacity – Move through hinge moments with courage

Alignment – Live in accordance with your values

Longevity – Build a life that widens, not narrows

This is the heart of this book: aging with agency and dignity.

9. Spiritual or Reflective Practice

Vitality – Notice what nourishes your inner life

Intention – Create space for reflection

Tenacity – Return to your practices even when life is full

Alignment – Live in accordance with your beliefs

Longevity – Build rituals that sustain meaning

Reflection becomes a steadying force.

10. Learning, Curiosity, and Growth

Vitality – Follow what sparks interest

Intention – Learn with purpose, not pressure

Tenacity – Stay with the process when it gets difficult

Alignment – Choose learning that supports who you want to become

Longevity – Cultivate a lifelong curiosity

In the "everything era," depth becomes a deliberate act.

The V.I.T.A.L. framework is not a prescription. It is a way of orienting yourself—a method for moving through life with clarity, steadiness, and dignity. Whether applied to the body, the mind, relationships, finances, or purpose, the principles remain the same:

Start small.

Move with intention.

Align with what matters.

Stay steady.

Build a life that lasts.

These applications are not endpoints but invitations—ways of carrying the pillars forward into the ordinary moments where life actually unfolds.

For Your Season

The V.I.T.A.L. pillars are not meant to be followed in sequence. They're touchpoints you can return to as your life shifts. If you're depleted, begin with Vitality. If you feel scattered, turn to Alignment. If you're rebuilding, Tenacity may meet you where you are. When you need direction, Intention offers clarity. And when you're thinking about the long arc of your life, Longevity widens the frame.

Use what serves you now. Let the rest wait until your season changes. This framework is here to move with you, not ahead of you.

INTRODUCTION TO THE V.I.T.A.L. MASTER GLOSSARY

The V.I.T.A.L. Master Glossary is more than a list of definitions—it is a bridge across disciplines. Some entries extend themes implied in the manuscript, offering additional metaphors and tools for reflection. Each term is presented through the lenses of photography, data science, and health/mind-body practice, showing how technical language transforms into living metaphors for intentional aging and resilience. By weaving together these perspectives, the glossary helps readers calibrate their own understanding: adjusting focus like a camera, refining inputs like a model, and tuning daily habits like the body's rhythms. Use this section as both a reference guide and a reflection tool—a place to revisit key concepts, reframe challenges, and carry forward the language of vitality, intention, tenacity, alignment, and longevity.

V.I.T.A.L. GLOSSARY—QUICK REFERENCE

The heart of this framework rests on five pillars: Vitality, Intention, Tenacity, Alignment, and Longevity. Together, they form the foundation for intentional aging and resilient living. Each pillar stands on its own, yet their true strength emerges when they are practiced in concert—energy directed with purpose, persistence balanced with coherence, and endurance shaped by legacy.

- **Vitality** – the energy reserves that fuel movement, creativity, and renewal.
- **Intention** – the clarity of focus that directs vitality toward meaningful outcomes.
- **Tenacity** – the persistence that steadies effort through challenge and change.
- **Alignment** – the balance between values, actions, and relationships that sustains coherence.

- **Longevity** – the perspective that honors endurance, legacy, and the quality of years lived with agency.

This Quick Reference offers readers a compass: a way to orient themselves to the language of the framework before exploring the deeper glossary. It is both a starting point and a reminder that hope is embodied in daily choices, agency is strengthened through practice, and dignity is carried forward when these pillars are lived intentionally.

Term	Photography	Data Science	Health/Mind-Body
Vitality	ISO / Sensor sensitivity—energy captured.	Data input quality—clean datasets fuel reliable models.	Physical energy reserves; sleep, nutrition, movement.
Intention	Aperture / Focus ring—sharpens subject, controls depth of field. The setting of the camera's compass: choosing aperture, angle, and subject before the shot is taken.	Feature selection—choosing variables to emphasize signal. The hypothesis or model design—the philosophical compass that defines what you seek to measure.	Mental clarity and purpose guiding choices. The values and desired course you set: the decision to train, rest, or live with purpose.
Tenacity	Tripod lock / long exposure stability—holding steady through instability.	Iterative training cycles—persistence through epochs builds resilience.	Emotional resilience, habit formation when motivation is low.

Term	Photography	Data Science	Health/Mind-Body
Alignment	Leading lines / level—balance and coherence in composition. The real-time integrity check: ensuring the lens, tripod, and horizon are actually lined up with the intended frame.	Model calibration—adjusting predictions to match reality. The sensor reading or validation step—comparing actual data against the intended model to confirm integrity.	Harmony between values, actions, and relationships. The daily practice check: actions, posture, and habits measured against the values you set.
Longevity	Long exposure—patience reveals hidden detail across time.	Generalization/dimensionality—sustaining performance across varied datasets, avoiding overfit.	Enduring perspective, legacy, sustained healthspan.

SYNERGIES (CONTINUOUS-LOOP RELATIONSHIPS)

The five pillars of Vitality, Intention, Tenacity, Alignment, and Longevity stand as the foundation of the V.I.T.A.L. framework. Yet their true strength emerges not in isolation but in the ways they connect and reinforce one another. This section highlights those synergies—the dynamic relationships where energy meets focus, persistence meets balance, and legacy meets endurance.

Just as in photography, where ISO, aperture, and shutter speed form a triangle of light, the pillars of V.I.T.A.L. form a living system. Each interaction reveals how resilience is built, how perspective is reframed, and how agency is sustained. These synergies remind us that intentional aging is not a solitary act but a continual calibration of forces working together.

Readers are invited to explore these connections not only as definitions but as guides for practice. They show how vitality can be directed with intention, how alignment can steady tenacity, and how longevity is nurtured through balance. In recognizing these relationships, we honor the dignity of a life lived with coherence—where hope is not abstract but embodied in the interplay of our choices.

These four are the conceptual backbone of V.I.T.A.L.—they describe how the framework sustains motion.

Additional pillar pairings and embodied micro-drills can be found in Appendix E: A Deeper Look at the V.I.T.A.L. Framework.

Synergy	Photography	Data Science	Health/Mind-Body
Vitality ↔ Intention (Energy ↔ Focus)	ISO (sensitivity) balanced with Aperture/Focus (clarity). Energy directed toward a chosen subject.	Input sensitivity tuned with model parameters. Raw data becomes meaningful when guided by purpose.	Energy reserves aligned with deliberate practice. Movement fueled by purpose rather than scattered effort.
Tenacity ↔ Alignment (Stability ↔ Flow)	Shutter Speed (persistence over time) paired with Level/Tripod (balance). Long exposure steadied by stability.	Iterative training cycles held steady by consistent calibration. Persistence without drift.	Endurance supported by posture and values. Effort sustained when aligned with what matters most.
Alignment ↔ Longevity (Balance ↔ Perspective)	A tripod's level and framing ensure stability across long exposures. Without alignment, even a well-timed shot blurs; with it, the image endures with clarity.	Long-term trend analysis depends on consistent calibration. When models stay aligned with core parameters, they avoid drift and remain reliable over time.	Posture, values, and daily practices aligned with purpose sustain longevity. A body and life in balance can carry endurance with dignity, ensuring that years are lived with coherence rather than fragmentation.

Synergy	Photography	Data Science	Health/Mind-Body
Intention ↔ Longevity (Focus ↔ Endurance)	Aperture and focus determine what endures in the frame. Intention directs the lens toward what matters most, ensuring that the captured image has lasting significance.	Purposeful parameter selection shapes which outputs remain meaningful over time. Intention guides longevity by filtering noise and preserving signal.	Clear goals and deliberate choices extend the quality of years lived. Intention provides direction so longevity is not just survival but a legacy of purposeful living.

The synergies remind us that the five pillars of Vitality, Intention, Tenacity, Alignment, and Longevity are not static points but living forces that continually shape one another. Energy without focus drifts; persistence without balance falters; endurance without purpose loses meaning. Yet when these elements interact, they create coherence—a framework where hope is sustained, agency is strengthened, and dignity is carried forward.

Just as a photograph is defined not only by its individual settings but by the harmony of ISO, aperture, and shutter speed, so too is a life defined by the interplay of its choices. These interactions are the calibration points of intentional aging, guiding us toward resilience and legacy.

With this foundation, you can now turn to the Supporting Terms and Metaphors, where the languages of photography, data science, and movement science expand the framework further. Together, the pillars and their synergies form the compass; the supporting terms provide the map.

SUPPORTING TERMS AND METAPHORS

While the Quick Reference highlights the five core pillars—Vitality, Intention, Tenacity, Alignment, and Longevity—the framework is enriched by a wider constellation of concepts. These Supporting Terms and Metaphors draw from photography, data science, and movement science to provide context, nuance, and practical imagery. They act as the connective tissue of the manuscript, helping readers see how the pillars operate in real life: how energy is captured, how focus is directed, how resilience is sustained, and how perspective is reframed. This section is designed as a deeper reference, offering readers both technical clarity and metaphorical resonance to carry forward into practice.

Term	Photography	Data Science	Health/Mind-Body
Adaptability	Adjusting exposure for changing light.	Updating models for new data distributions.	Flexibility in routines and responses to change.
Adaptive Load	Adjusting aperture.	Shifting parameters.	Scaling effort to capacity.
Anchor Line	A compositional element that grounds the frame.	A baseline or reference variable anchoring analysis.	Foundational habits that stabilize daily life.
Aperture	Lens opening controlling depth of field and focus.	Feature selection—choosing variables to emphasize signal.	Mental focus; narrowing priorities to reduce overwhelm.
Bias/ Variance	Tilted horizon vs. blurred image.	Underfitting vs. overfitting tension.	Skewed habits vs. unstable routines.
Calibration Flow	Adjusting exposure settings in sequence for balance.	Workflow of tuning models step by step.	Iterative adjustments in routines to maintain equilibrium.

Term	Photography	Data Science	Health/Mind-Body
Continuity Arc	The sweep of a panorama or sequence of frames, connecting beginnings to endings in one continuous line of vision.	A long-term trend line that reveals how patterns persist and evolve, linking past data to future projections.	The trajectory of intentional aging, where daily practices accumulate into a life aligned with values and resilience.
Continuous Calibration	Adjusting ISO, aperture, and exposure in real time.	Ongoing retraining to adapt to new data streams.	Daily adjustments in habits, routines, and mindset.
Cropping/ Framing	Choosing what to include/exclude in the shot.	Defining dataset boundaries.	Setting healthy boundaries in relationships and commitments.
Deferred Maintenance	Neglecting lens cleaning or calibration until distortion appears.	Postponing model retraining or updates, leading to drift.	Ignoring small issues until they accumulate into larger problems.
Dimensionality	Multiple compositional elements—lines, light, depth.	Number of features in a dataset; too many can obscure clarity.	Complexity of mind-body interactions requiring balance.
Embodied Hinge	The pivot of a tripod or lens mount, where stability meets flexibility, allowing the frame to shift without losing focus.	The inflection point in a dataset, where a curve bends and reveals transition—capturing both continuity and change.	The joint that enables movement and resilience, balancing strength with adaptability so the body can pivot without breaking.
Emotional Contagion	The spread of light or color across an image, where one tone influences the mood of the whole frame.	Signal propagation—how one variable or anomaly can ripple through a dataset or network.	The unconscious transmission of emotions between people; "catching" stress, joy, or calm from others.

Term	Photography	Data Science	Health/Mind-Body
EXIF Metadata	EXIF (exchangeable image file format) metadata is the hidden information stored in image files—camera model, lens, aperture, shutter speed, ISO, date/time, and sometimes GPS location. It's the backstory of a photo, invisible to the eye but essential for context.	Equivalent to metadata in datasets—information about how data was collected, processed, or structured. Without metadata, interpretation can be misleading. It's the "audit trail" that ensures transparency and reproducibility.	A metaphor for the hidden context behind daily states—sleep quality, stress levels, nutrition, or environment. Just as EXIF reveals unseen details of a photo, health metadata (like HRV, RHR, or proprioception signals) reveals the unseen factors shaping vitality.
Focus Ring	Manual adjustment to sharpen the subject.	Fine-tuning feature selection or hyperparameters.	Mental focus—directing attention to what matters most.
Generational Aperture	The opening through which one generation's light passes to the next, shaping exposure and focus.	The observation window that reveals how patterns shift across cohorts, connecting past datasets to future trends.	The span of influence across life stages, where values and practices are transmitted through intentional aging.
Healthspan	Exposure triangle (ISO, aperture, shutter speed) – balance of settings for optimal image.	Performance metrics (accuracy, precision, recall).	Quality of years lived with agency, not just quantity.

Term	Photography	Data Science	Health/Mind-Body
Hinge Generation	The hinge is the pivot point of a lens or shutter—where movement allows light to enter and create the image. The Hinge Generation is like that pivot, connecting past exposures with future frames.	A hinge is the inflection point in a dataset, where the curve bends and trends shift. The Hinge Generation represents that turning point in collective data—where legacy patterns meet new trajectories.	The hinge is the joint—knees, hips, shoulders—that allows movement and transition. The Hinge Generation embodies the role of carrying weight while enabling forward motion across life stages.
HRV (Heart Rate Variability)	N/A	Variability metric akin to variance in datasets.	Measure of autonomic nervous system balance; resilience indicator.
ISO	Sensor sensitivity; too high = noise, too low = dim.	Input variability; noisy or incomplete data reduces clarity.	Responsiveness of energy reserves; how quickly the body reacts to stress or recovery.
Leading Lines	Compositional guides that direct the eye.	Structured flows guiding interpretation.	Values and routines that direct daily choices.
Legacy Lens	Wide-angle perspective capturing horizon and continuity.	Long-term trend analysis.	Looking beyond immediate outcomes to enduring impact.
Lens Shift	Tilt-shift adjustment; changes perspective without moving the camera, correcting distortion.	Re-parameterization or reframing of variables; correcting bias or distortion.	Mental reframing or posture adjustment; shifting perspective to restore balance.
Level	Tool ensuring horizons are balanced and straight.	Calibration—aligning predictions with reality.	Emotional and physical balance; keeping perspective steady.

Term	Photography	Data Science	Health/Mind-Body
Living Archive	The evolving collection of images and albums, where memory is not static but continually reframed.	A dynamic repository of data, updated and reinterpreted over time, reflecting both history and ongoing change.	The embodied record of experience—habits, movements, and resilience stored in the body and carried forward through intentional practice.
Long Exposure	Extended shutter time revealing hidden detail and motion trails.	Generalization across time—models that sustain accuracy on unseen data.	Patience and endurance; practices that reveal deeper meaning over time.
Micro-recoveries	The brief reset between exposures.	The recalibration of a model.	The breath that restores balance.
Mindfulness	Intentional composition; noticing light and detail.	Monitoring model drift carefully.	Awareness of present moment; reducing stress and reactivity.
Overfit	Over-editing an image until it loses authenticity.	Model too tailored to training data, failing on new inputs.	Rigid routines that collapse when life shifts.
Proprioception	N/A	Sensor feedback loops in robotics or modeling.	Body's awareness of position and movement; foundation of balance and coordination.
Quiet Agency	The subtle act of framing or adjusting light without drawing attention, shaping meaning through restraint.	Small, precise adjustments to parameters or models that shift outcomes without dramatic disruption.	Gentle, intentional practices—like breathing, stretching, or resting—that reclaim balance without fanfare.

Term	Photography	Data Science	Health/Mind-Body
Resilience	Recovering from poor lighting or unstable conditions.	Model robustness against noisy data.	Emotional strength to rebound from setbacks.
Resonant Pause	The intentional use of negative space or stillness in an image, where silence amplifies meaning.	The gap between signals or data points that highlights patterns more clearly than constant input.	A mindful moment of rest or breath that restores balance, allowing renewal and deeper resilience.
Reverse the Logic of Deferral	Instead of waiting for the "perfect light," you shoot now—capturing the moment as it is. The reversal is choosing presence over postponement.	Instead of deferring analysis until more data arrives, you act on the current dataset—iterating and refining. The reversal is agency in the face of uncertainty.	Instead of deferring exercise or care until "later," you move now—stretch, breathe, act. The reversal is reclaiming agency by prioritizing immediate practice over indefinite delay.
RHR (Resting Heart Rate)	N/A	Baseline metric; starting point for model evaluation.	Indicator of cardiovascular fitness and recovery capacity.
Rolleiflex	Emotion is a Rolleiflex—twin-lensed and deliberate. One lens sees, the other remembers. It doesn't just record; it witnesses.	Emotion is a signal in the dataset—an outlier that shifts the model, the metadata that gives numbers meaning.	Emotion is breath in motion—rising and falling, restoring flow, the rhythm that connects mind and body.
Selective Focus	Technique of isolating subject by blurring background.	Dimensionality reduction—emphasizing key variables.	Concentrating on what matters most, filtering distractions.

Term	Photography	Data Science	Health/Mind-Body
Sensor	The heart of the camera, capturing light and detail.	Raw data input—the foundation of any model.	Body's sensory systems; awareness of signals like fatigue, stress, or vitality.
Shadow Drift	The gradual encroachment of darkness at the edges of a frame, where light quietly recedes without notice.	The subtle bias or missing values that creep into a dataset over time, shifting outcomes without overt disruption.	The unnoticed decline in self-care or resilience, where small omissions accumulate until imbalance emerges.
Shutter Speed	Duration of exposure; fast = freeze, slow = blur.	Training pace; speed of iterations affects stability.	Pacing of effort; balancing bursts of activity with rest.
Silent Surrender of Self-Care	The underexposed frame—light was available, but the aperture closed too soon. Self-care fades quietly, leaving shadows where brightness could have been.	A gradual drift in the dataset—small anomalies go unflagged, thresholds loosen, and signal degrades into noise. Self-care erodes not through a single failure, but through unmonitored variance that quietly shifts the baseline.	Neglecting rest or hydration—small omissions that accumulate. The surrender is silent, but the body eventually signals imbalance.
Three Planes of Motion	N/A	N/A	Sagittal (forward/back), frontal (side/side), transverse (rotation). metaphor for multidimensional living and adaptability.
Tripod Lock	Mechanism that stabilizes the camera during long exposures.	Anchoring iterative training to prevent instability.	Emotional grounding and physical stability—habits that hold steady under pressure.

FINAL REFLECTION

There is a moment, after any long journey, when you set the camera down and realize the image you were trying to capture has already taken shape inside you—not as a single frame but as a series of small exposures. Movements, choices, hesitations, and recoveries reveal who you've become along the way. This final reflection is a pause to notice that unfolding and to sense what you're ready to carry forward into your own life.

This book began in a season when my world narrowed to a pinhole. I wrote to steady myself, to understand what was breaking and what was quietly rebuilding. But somewhere in the writing, the frame widened. What started as survival became practice. What began as crisis became clarity. And what felt like an ending became a hinge.

If you've read this far, you've carried your own questions through these pages. You've paused, noticed, tested, returned. You've traced the contours of your life with a little more honesty, a little more patience, a little more breath. That is its own kind of courage.

V.I.T.A.L. was never meant to be a doctrine. It is a way of seeing—one that invites you to move with intention, to honor your energy, to stay steady in the blur, to align with what matters, and to build a life that can hold you for the long exposure. You don't need to master it. You only need to practice it in the smallest possible ways.

As you step beyond these pages, may you trust the movements that feel true. May you give yourself permission to recalibrate when the light shifts. May you remember that clarity is not a destination but a rhythm—one you return to again and again.

And may you carry forward the quiet knowing that your story is still unfolding, and you are already shaping it.

I began in the margins, unsure if there was room to speak.

I close with gratitude—

for the space, the ink, and the courage to write.

May you find your own margins wide enough to hold hope

and your own story bold enough to be told.